SON OF
FORGOTTEN HOLLYWOOD
FORGOTTEN HISTORY

Starring More Great Character Actors
of Hollywood's Golden Age

MANNY PACHECO

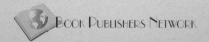
BOOK PUBLISHERS NETWORK

Book Publishers Network
P.O. Box 2256
Bothell • WA • 98041
Ph • 425-483-3040
www.bookpublishersnetwork.com

10 9 8 7 6 5 4 3 2 1
Printed in the United States of America

LCCN 2011942509
ISBN   978-1-937454-14-2

Editor: Barbara Kindness
Cover Designer: Nina Barnett
Typographer: Stephanie Martindale

CONTENTS

FOREWORD

BY DAVID C. BOJORQUEZ

WHAT MAKES THIS MEDIA PROPERTY—*Forgotten Hollywood Forgotten History*—compelling for us are the stories behind some of the most beloved movies and cinematic legends from Hollywood's Golden Era, and how many of these true accounts are surprisingly relevant for our times.

Within this rich, untold history of Hollywood lies a treasure trove of great and poignant social commentary. As an example, one of the documentary segments we use from the first book in the series focuses on Ward Bond's misguided zealousness to expose actors suspected of 'anti-American,' Communist activities during the McCarthy era. This seldom-told, true story provides

Senator Joseph McCarthy

a perfect allegorical background to the terrorist fear-mongering we face today, and the civil rights abuses which have become way too prevalent since 9/11.

Younger viewers especially will discover that none of the issues we wrestle with in the twenty-first century are new. ***Forgotten Hollywood*** is a powerful moving allegory to the greatest challenges we are still wrestling with today—from immigration, to race relations, to even the rights of the disabled. And, our goal here is not to be didactic, but simply to relate the untold stories of the actors, directors, and movies from a 'forgotten' Hollywood era that, when revealed, suddenly become powerful reminders of how much work we have left to do.

President George H. W. Bush signs the Americans with Disabilities Act of 1990 into law.

Social commentary is nothing new in motion pictures. Movies have always served as both a mirror and a barometer to the consciousness of our nation. And if we do our job right, my hope is that our movie project (like Manny Pacheco's words in his books) encourages dialogue vital to creating a more united, compassionate world.

I just want to compliment Manny on both his historical and Hollywood knowledge, as well as the immense amount of in-depth research he conducted in putting his book-series together. It's truly monumental work. They are very well written, and certainly reflect a man with a definitive passion for his subject matter. As I continue to read his books, it's an ongoing WOW! for me.

David C. Bojorquez,
President, Vision4Media

PREFACE

I HAD A HUNCH THE UNITED STATES was ready for a book that told America's story through the eyes of forgotten Hollywood character actors during its Golden Age. What really surprised me was the success of my first book (and even getting it published in the first place). The journey on which *Forgotten Hollywood Forgotten History* has taken me includes historic landmarks, a variety of festivals, the sadly diminishing world of book-buying, and a constant return back to cinema's past.

Sherlock Holmes
(illustration)

Vision4Media, a Brea, California production company slated my stories for a documentary to be distributed as a domestic and international theatrical film and/

New Orleans Mardi Gras, Proteus parade float with Robin Hood theme *(drawing)*

or cable television series. This was exciting news! Moreover, it's gratifying to see current filmmakers remake classic movies featuring such unforgettable characters as *Sherlock Holmes*, *Robin Hood*, and *The Wolfman*. Time will tell how historically significant these motion pictures are in bringing these tales to the current generation of filmgoers and critics.

My initial starting point was at the Richard Nixon Library in Yorba Linda, where I found my publisher, Book Publishers Network, quite by accident. This highly professional business was promoting Ed Nixon, the former president's younger brother, and unveiling his new book on President's Day, 2009. This gave my wife, Laurie, and me a glimpse at how successful a book signing appearance could be. It was at the Nixon Library where I met Mr. Nixon and Sheryn Hara, owner of her Washington State-based publishing group. Hara assured me my book would receive BPN consideration with regard to helping me self-publish my material, printing, distribution, and its subsequent marketing. After later convincing Hara of my sincere intention of aggressively sending a nostalgic message through my words, I was accepted into the Network.

My next stop involved a chance encounter with Gary Lycan of the *Orange County Register* at a Southern California radio reunion. Several conversations led to his writing a heartfelt *Foreword* for the book. Lycan has joined me on this trip down motion pictures' beloved past, and he has feverishly guided my steps toward success. His contributions have been invaluable in getting my book into the appropriate hands. It was Lycan who first believed it belonged at the Paley Center for Media (formerly the Television and Radio Museum) in Beverly Hills; the prestigious shelves of the Academy of Motion Picture Arts and Sciences' Margaret Herrick Library; the American Film Institute's Louis B. Mayer Library; and the Writer's Guild Foundation's Shavelson-Webb Library.

He also was committed to seeing my paperback sold along Hollywood Boulevard. His dedication helped me convince the historic Roosevelt Hotel to initially consider **Forgotten Hollywood Forgotten History** for their gift shop. The hotel was the actual site of the first Academy Awards ceremony. The Hollywood Heritage Museum is the latest iconic locale to carry my work. I'm proud to have collaborated with Gary Lycan in this book series. He has written a magnificent *Introduction* to this particular paperback.

Roosevelt Hotel in Hollywood, CA

My family, including Laurie, Virginia (Vigi), Matthew, Mark, Maxime, and, of course, my parents (Manuel & Gloria) worked on the traditional means of book distribution. What followed was a state-of-the-art website at www.forgottenhollywood.com, YouTube videos, Twitter and Facebook accounts, and a ground-game with word-of-mouth sales that astonished my professional marketing team. My media-savvy circle, part of Book Publishers Network, including Ms. Hara, Stephanie Martindale, and Laura Danforth, also worked hard at making sure my product was available on Amazon.com, in a number of Barnes & Noble bookstores, and at international independent book sellers. Newspaper press, television and radio interviews, and five-star book reviews helped our cause immeasurably. The positive impact of my campaign has led to the USA Book News presenting **Forgotten Hollywood Forgotten History** a 2009 Best Book Award. More national awards emerged. A recent accolade has come from the international World Book Awards (as a gold medal recipient). I now host a weekly show with Gary Lycan called *Forgotten Hollywood* on *The Spa* radio network that can be heard at: http://tuner1.dc1.sonix-tream.com/playlists/am1510kspa/am1510kspaKSPAAM.asx.

USA Best Book Awards *(seal)*

My friends in business have also offered their help in ensuring the success of my initial work. The entire Southern California karaoke community (*it seems*) has supporting me financially by purchasing copies of my book. Peter Parker and *Karaoke Scene Magazine* created the opportunity to see that my paperback ended up in the hands of the staff of Harpo Productions. Tim Keenan of Creative Media and Russ Duke of KNR Entertainment have helped me implement modern ideas to network and market my product. Supporters from the radio and television community, the Buena Park Moose Lodge (local site of my official national charity), and even my bowling league, have additionally shared in the enthusiastic response to my book.

Tim Keenan, former mayor of Cypress, CA

I can proudly say that actors Hugh O'Brian, Edward James Olmos, Theodore Bikel, Jane Withers, and the creative teams of the Jim Henson Company and Florentine Films (home to Ken Burns), have spent an evening or two with Hollywood's forgotten stars. And, this list has grown to include Emmy winners, Oscar nominees, members of the Radio Hall of Fame, and even an eight-time former congressman. Of course, the youngest brother of a former US President also owns a copy of **Forgotten Hollywood Forgotten History**. I guess we have come full circle.

The tireless efforts by my entire entourage have continued while I've been busy hatching part two, and as I blog on a semi-daily basis on my website. What started

Manny Pacheco and Ed Nixon
at Portland Book Fair *(2009)*

as a literary niche has snowballed into a minor phenomenon. This positive reaction has confirmed my desire to write a sequel (with twenty-one memorable stories). I'm gratified generations of folks, now worldwide, have a desire to affectionately remember our cherished past. With a little luck, my small success story might be recognized as important within the framework of our current American landscape. Either way, let's once again visit a gentler, ambitious, often tumultuous—and may I remind you—sometimes forgotten era of our forefathers in American and Hollywood history.

Cesar Romero

Gilbert Roland

INTRODUCTION

BY GARY LYCAN

YOU ARE ABOUT TO START on your road trip into the land of *Forgotten Hollywood*. The first book took us on a journey into the theaters of the '30s, '40s and '50s where motion pictures were part of "double features"—meaning you saw an "A" movie and a "B" movie on the bill, plus popcorn and a drink for less than fifty cents. It's often forgotten that cinema ticket prices averaged twenty-four cents. According to the Motion Picture Association of America (MPAA), it wasn't until 1965 that the average film ticket price rose above a dollar.

Manny Pacheco's books—and we can expect more in this series—are, in a way, his director's cut. He focuses his lens on character actors who were key players in movie storylines, but few people remember their names today. And, taking on the director's role, he is neither historian nor biographer. He is a storyteller, sharing with us his revelations on how these character actors often played real-life historical roles. He feeds our curiosity, touches our heart, and nourishes our spirit. And it opens our eyes to a greater appreciation of those *"what's their name"* performers whom we can rediscover today thanks to re-mastered films on DVD, on the Fox Movie Channel and Turner Classic Movies.

Forgotten Hollywood Forgotten History is not about movies per se. It's about the memories created by classic movies. And it may spark your interest in other forgotten people, places and things that tie Hollywood to history. How many films, for example, poked fun at or used in scenes those Burma Shave signs that populated the highway landscape. You know the ones that said such things as: *"She Kissed the Hairbrush / By Mistake / She Thought It Was / Her Husband Jake / Burma Shave."* Or this one: *"Little Bo Peep / Was Driving Her Jeep / She Fell Asleep / Now's Counting Sheep / Burma Shave."*

Set of signs promoting Burma-Shave on US Route 66

If this book fascinates you, enjoy discovering these other "forgotten" film treasures:

- The music of composer Johnny Mercer (*"Laura," "On the Atchison, Topeka and the Santa Fe," "Button up Your Overcoat,"* and hundreds of other standards).

- Robert and Richard Sherman, the lyricist and composer team who wrote more motion picture musical scores than any other songwriting tandem in film history, including *"It's*

Richard and Robert Sherman

a Small World"; the **Mary Poppins** score that included the Oscar-winning "*Chim-Chim-Cheree*" and "*Super-califragilisticexpialidocious*"; the theme to **Winnie the Pooh**; and even "*Tall Paul*" for Annette Funicello. If you have been to Disneyland in Anaheim, California, you hear their music in *The Enchanted Tiki Room*. No wonder they got their own window on *Main Street USA* in 2010.

- *Griffith Park tops the 2010 list of LA's busiest film locations,* according to FilmLA Inc. Other popular movie-making sites are Venice, the 6ᵗʰ Street Bridge, Will Rogers State Park, Dockweiler Beach, the 2ⁿᵈ Street Tunnel, Point Dume, and Elysian Park. How often have you watched a scene and said to yourself, "*That looks so familiar. I wonder where they filmed it.*"

Point Dume, Malibu, CA

- Sedona and Northern Arizona were location sites for more than sixty Hollywood productions from the first years of the movies into the 1970s. A book called **Arizona's Little Hollywood** reveals the area's forgotten film history from 1923 to 1973. Among its gems: the details on the filming of John Ford's **Stagecoach**" and **Johnny Guitar**, and the story of the historical importance of 1950's **Broken Arrow** for its role in the fight against the Hollywood Blacklist.

- Recognize the name Norman Rockwell? If not, you might remember all those magazine covers gracing *The Saturday Evening Post* (and other notable magazines). What was unknown until recently was that Rockwell's oil paintings were collected by filmmakers Steven Spielberg and George

Norman Rockwell

Popular Science Magazine *(cover depicting inventor imagining perpetual motion)*

President and Mrs. Reagan and Steven Spielberg at a White House film screening

Lucas because each man was so impressed with how Rockwell cast and directed people to create the scenes he would use to produce his paintings. Spielberg said he had a Rockwell scene in mind when shooting a crowd scene in **Close Encounters of the Third Kind**;

Clark Gable/Mutiny on the Bounty
(trailer)

Mutiny on the Bounty *(trailer)*

and one of his scenes in **Empire of the Sun** positioned the actors with the same pose as in a Rockwell painting. Who knew Rockwell's work would find new life in the movies?

- My mother Mary grew up in Hollywood, and she would pass down stories that might otherwise have been forgotten. She would tell me (and photos prove it) of the time she was at the beach on Catalina Island, looking down at her camera, then looking up and seeing Clark Gable, all by himself, walking in the sand a few hundred feet away. He saw her, could tell she wanted to take a photo, and just stood there quietly so she could take her picture. He was filming **Mutiny on the Bounty** for MGM. She also recalled how the great character actress Mary Astor lived up the

Mary Astor/The Hurricane
(trailer)

street, and whenever she was outside playing on the front lawn and Astor drove by in her Cord convertible, the actress would press the horn with its "ooga-ooga" sound and wave to her.

- You can find *Forgotten Hollywood* history in Orange County, California, at Laguna Beach's Three Arch Bay. A family compound put on the housing market in 2010 is one of seven lots originally part of the D.W. Griffith Estate, and originally owned by Hollywood screenwriters in the 1920s.

- In the "did you know" film category, we lost in 2010 Ilene Woods, who was the voice of *Cinderella* in Disney's animated classic. Ann Rutherford (*Careen* in **Gone with the Wind** and *Polly* in the **Andy Hardy** movies) was still talking about Hollywood's Golden Age—and her career— in 2009 at age 89. And if you really want to know anything about Hollywood movie history, the "go to" person is A.C. Lyles, a former Paramount movie producer. You don't know his name, but in 2010, at age 92, this strikingly handsome man could still tell stories.

Anne Rutherford/Love Finds Andy Hardy *(trailer)*

Southern California television personality Ralph Story did two excellent PBS documentaries on **Things That Aren't Here Anymore**. And that's the point. The people profiled in the following chapters are no longer with us, but thanks to Manny Pacheco's storytelling vision and insights, we create memories from their movies, and we see and appreciate Hollywood history in a new light, and the afterglow brightens our hope there will be more stories to come. So, sit back, take your time, and start your journey into **Forgotten Hollywood Forgotten History**.

Gary Lycan
Radio Columnist, *Orange County Register*
Executive Producer and Co-Host, **The Pet Place** Television Show

CHAPTER ONE

FAT MAN AND LITTLE BOY

Sydney Greenstreet (1879-1954)
Peter Lorre (1904-1964)

ONE ACTOR WAS DIMINUTIVE AND ODDLY MENACING, the other rotund and robust. Both film stars may have been the most successful screen duo this side of Spencer Tracy and Katharine Hepburn. The story of Sydney Greenstreet and Peter Lorre in cinema remains one of international intrigue and mystery. They were also inadvertently joined together by the grim solution that ultimately ended World War II. Either way, it's one heck of a story.

Born in England, Sydney Greenstreet didn't turn to acting right away. His failure as a Ceylon tea planter and brewery manager forced his hand. He first appeared on stage as a villain in a *Sherlock Holmes* stage play in

Sydney Greenstreet and Peter Lorre/
The Maltese Falcon *(trailer)*

1902. He spent the next four decades performing in a variety of Shakespearean and musical comedy productions on both sides of the Atlantic. He was cast in the Broadway production **Roberta**, which made Bob Hope a star. Also featured were George Murphy, Fred Mac-Murray, and the music of Jerome Kern. The show introduced a little number that became an instant standard—*Smoke Gets in Your Eyes*.

Bob Hope

Greenstreet was way past middle age in his film debut, and his career lasted only eight years. Not many actors can boast a first motion picture appearance at age sixty-two. He co-starred in a scant twenty-three films, nine with Peter Lorre. When he finally accepted a contract with Warner Brothers, the movie studio found Greenstreet to be a ready-made villain for movie mysteries that centered on international espionage. This was a convenient plot line, considering the United States teetered on the brink of war during this time.

The Maltese Falcon is a detective potboiler written by Dashiell Hammett, starring Humphrey Bogart as the memorable *Sam Spade*. The movie, generally regarded as the first *film noir* entry into the genre, featured Mary Astor, Elisha Cook, Jr., and Lorre. Greenstreet was the head of this menacing quartet in search of a rare black bird statue and they stopped at nothing (including murder) to retrieve the valuable prize. Director John Huston captured the essence of the duplicitous nature of hero and villain. Sydney Greenstreet played his part in a broad comedic fashion, making the movie all the more fun. It's also obvious that chemistry existed between the nervous Lorre and the portly Greenstreet. And his role as *Kasper Gutman "The Fat Man"* was good enough to earn him an Oscar nomination in 1941.

Greenstreet was just ok in **They Died with Their Boots On** and **Across the Pacific**. Despite the fact that he was reunited with Bogart and Astor in the latter film, his characters were simply not definitive Greenstreet. The next film role, however, cemented his on-screen reputation as a jovial miscreant. The cinema classic **Casablanca** remains more than just a love story. It's a tale of survival in the worst of situations. The movie portrays this godforsaken corner of the world as home to a variety of folks swept up in the Nazi campaign for domination in North Africa. A number of the characters spend much of the pic-

Sydney Greensteet and Humphrey Bogart/Casablanca *(trailer)*

ture looking for a chance to escape. The survivors of the locale are determined to exist discreetly without getting in the way of a pesky war that has disrupted their lives. Bogart and Greenstreet play rival owners of saloons, content not to interfere with the daily struggles for freedom. Greenstreet's *Signor Ferrari* is a fez-wearing, fly-swatting gent who's not above making money off *Casablanca's* most valuable commodity—human life. Peter Lorre and Greenstreet never share screen time. But this film solidified the pairing of the two actors as a cinematic team by the heads of Warner Brothers. They were motion pictures' first "odd couple."

They appeared in seven more movies including **Passage to Marseille**, **The Mask of Dimitrios**, **Three Strangers**, **Background to Danger**, and **The Verdict**. They also had a sinister-parody cameo in the film tribute to **The Hollywood Canteen** (as themselves). In fact, Greenstreet donated his off-screen time at *The Canteen* by cooking and serving food for soldiers on leave. Admission was

Hollywood Canteen

free for servicemen. Many stars spent much of World War II as "ambassadors" at *The Canteen*, an actual patriotic brainchild of Bette Davis and John Garfield.

After the war, Sydney Greenstreet co-starred in important pictures. Among the films— **Christmas in Connecticut**, **The**

Hucksters, with Clark Gable and Adolphe Menjou, *Flamingo Road,* starring Joan Crawford, and his final film, *Malaya*, featuring Spencer Tracy and James Stewart in their only screen time together. Greenstreet was forced to retire in order to battle diabetes.

Peter Lorre was a Hungarian born in Czechoslovakia, and lived in Vienna as a child. He studied with Sigmund Freud during his youth. He starred at age twenty-six in the sensational Fritz Lang film *M* (Lorre's second movie) in 1931. Despite his heavy accent, Alfred Hitchcock is credited for giving him his first English-speaking role in the 1934 British version of *The Man Who Knew Too Much*, and two years later in *Secret Agent*. During the 1930's, his Jewish family, now living in Germany, hated the rise of the Nazi Party. He later immigrated to the United States, and became a naturalized American citizen in 1936.

Director Fritz Lang and his wife in Berlin (circa 1923 or 1924)

Lorre had a much longer film résumé than Sydney Greenstreet. Columbia Pictures signed the actor to his first studio movie contract, and he was cast playing foreign sinister types. Lorre broke from this typecasting when given the chance to star as Japanese detective *Mr. Moto* in a number of movies. He was Warner Brothers' answer to *Charlie Chan*. When Lorre appeared in *The Maltese Falcon* as *Joel Cairo*, he became an instantly recognizable star with his banjo eyes, unmistakable voice, and twitchy behavior. He reprised his chilling role in *M* on radio. And, his small part in *Casablanca* as the doomed *Ugarte* secured the rest of his career.

Lorre was particularly memorable in *Arsenic and Old Lace* as *Dr. Einstein*, Raymond Massey's villainous friend with no stomach for murder. Massey resembled Boris Karloff in the film production.

In fact, Karloff might have played the part had he been available, ironically performing the same role on Broadway. A reference to the resemblance is a running gag throughout the picture. Director Frank Capra went all out casting this most successful stage play-turned-film classic. Cary Grant, Priscilla Lane, Jack Carson, James Gleason, Josephine Hull, and Edward Everett Horton were all

Peter Lorre's application for US citizenship

exceptional in their roles. However, the little-known John Alexander almost steals the movie as Grant's brother who thinks he's President Theodore Roosevelt. The Warner Brothers' movie was produced in 1941, but not released until 1944 per a contractual agreement with the stage promoters. Lorre was right at home in Capra's picture.

Adept at playing broad humor in dark and suspenseful movies, he co-starred in **All Through the Night** (again with Humphrey Bogart), and in the mystery comedy **My Favorite Brunette**. The latter film featured Bob Hope as an

Raymond Massey/Arsenic and Old Lace (trailer)

inept detective and Dorothy Lamour as a *femme fatale*. Alan Ladd and Bing Crosby had cameo roles, providing Hope the chance to parody *film noir* and promote his popular *Road* pictures. **Beat the Devil** is another example of Lorre's wry ability in a tongue-in-cheek reworking of **The Maltese Falcon**. The movie starred Bogart and was directed by John Huston. When Sydney Greenstreet refused to come out of retirement, Robert Morley assumed his role. Lorre also has the unique distinction of playing *James Bond*'s first screen adversary in a television adaptation of **Casino Royale** in 1954.

Lorre also excelled in the science fiction genre. He spent much of the fifties and sixties in movies that were screenplays of Jules Verne's books including **20,000 Leagues Under the Sea**, **Around the World in Eighty Days**, and **Five Weeks in a Balloon**; while in **The Story of Mankind**, he was utterly campy as *Nero*. The film featured an ensemble cast that starred Vincent Price as *The Devil*, Ronald Colman, and all three Marx Brothers (in separate segments). Lorre also appeared with Walter Pidgeon in **Voyage to the Bottom of the Sea** in a rare turn as an obedient and loyal confidante. Lorre was equally comfortable in horror cinema. In **The Beast with Five Fingers**, **Tales of Terror**, **The Raven**, and **Comedy of Terrors**, he held his own with Price, Boris Karloff, and Basil Rathbone in these gothic tales.

Vincent Price

A good friend to Vincent Price, they both attended the funeral of Bela Lugosi in 1956. In his will, Lugosi requested to be buried in his vampire cape. During the service, Lorre deviously suggested to "*drive a stake through (Lugosi's) heart—just in case!*" After Peter Lorre died in 1964, Price offered a moving eulogy.

Ironically, Sydney Greenstreet and Peter Lorre would be immortalized in history apart from their cinematic careers. While the United States was fighting two campaigns during World War II, Franklin D. Roosevelt grimaced at the prospect of a ground invasion into Tokyo. Albert Einstein first wrote FDR in 1939 about the idea of using atomic energy as a way of protecting our country. Einstein later regretted sending the letter, becoming a lifelong dissident over its eventual use.

Albert Einstein letter to President Franklin D. Roosevelt *(1939)*

By 1942, the President responded to the potential fear of Germany dabbling with the creation of atomic weaponry. He ordered the creation of *The Manhattan Project* under the direction of American physicist J. Robert Oppenheimer. The program looked at nuclear power as a way to fight Axis fascism in Europe and Asia, and a potential Russian threat that might loom after the war. Uranium enrichment was the key to harnessing energy used in a bomb. Italian physicist Enrico Fermi took the credit as the scientist creating the properties of fission energy needed for the internal workings of an atomic device. Incidentally, Fermi's wife was Jewish and both were targeted enemies of Benito Mussolini's Italy. They just escaped imprisonment by taking a spontaneous trip to Switzerland. Enrico and his wife then traveled to the United States and became naturalized citizens in 1944. Many city sites worked in secret under the direction of President

J. Robert Oppenheimer, first director of Los Alamos National Laboratory

Roosevelt, but it was at Los Alamos in New Mexico where the atomic bomb became a reality.

A student of Oppenheimer, Robert Serber created the code words for the weaponry. There were actually three atomic bombs created, and their monikers were reportedly based on the writings of Dashiell Hammett. The long-range device was called *The Thin Man* named after the successful detective novel. *Fat Man* and *Little Boy* were so-named in reference to the roles played by Greenstreet and Lorre in **The Maltese Falcon**. Others wanted to credit the nicknames as homage to British Prime Minister Winston Churchill and President Roosevelt, but Serber

Enrico Fermi, Italian-American physicist (received the 1938 Nobel Prize in physics for identifying new elements and discovering nuclear reactions by his method of nuclear irradiation and bombardment)

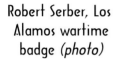

Robert Serber, Los Alamos wartime badge *(photo)*

A mockup of "The Fat Man" atomic device

dismissed this over the course of his life. In fact, the look of each bomb may have led to their selected nomenclature. They were the weaponry authorized for use by President Harry Truman after he was made aware of Roosevelt's research directive. The detonation of these devices across the Pacific became an attractive alternative to the proposed ground invasion into Tokyo. Scientists argued a million Allied lives over the course of a year might be instantly saved.

The Atomic Age in practice was born on August 6, 1945 when the *Enola Gay* (a B-29 bomber piloted by Col. Paul Tibbits) dropped *Little Boy* on Hiroshima. After *Fat Man* unloaded on Nagasaki three days later, Japan surrendered, thus ending World War II. The inevitable Cold War cautiously benefited the United States, which emerged as a superpower. However, the ultimate legacy of Hiroshima and Nagasaki remains the lasting impact of underlying global fear over every generation since 1945. The "genie out of the bottle" of hard lessons learned regarding the responsibility

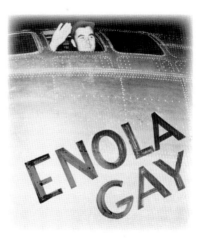

Paul Tibbets, pilot of Enola Gay, before the atomic attack on Hiroshima

of atomic energy use and the chance of our future enemy's development of cataclysmic nuclear devices live on into this century. Scientists in Los Alamos work to this day in a concerted effort to fight international terrorism.

Sydney Greenstreet and Peter Lorre might find all of this "terrorist talk" wickedly funny. These two character actors often faced down betrayal, deception, and espionage in many of the parts they played. They are a celluloid testament of

Atomic bombing of Nagasaki on August 9, 1945

human bravado and a lingering example of our ongoing collective will to survive on this planet.

Sydney Greenstreet and Peter Lorre/
The Hollywood Canteen (trailer)

FAT MAN AND LITTLE BOY

CHAPTER TWO

THE MAN BEHIND THE CURTAIN

Frank Morgan (1890-1949)

A STUDIO ACTOR'S LIFE could be so unfair. Once you embarked on your chosen profession, one might stumble in a variety of ways. Even a successful career forced typecasting. You either obeyed the rules laid down by your contract, or you were banished to lesser roles in unimportant movies. If you were lucky or smart enough to do everything right, the reward was steady work in choice assignments.

The story of Frank Morgan is one of talent, measured opportunities, and a valued place at Metro-Goldwyn-Mayer. However, he constantly battled so as not to exist in the shadow of others. His brother had a smaller career; yet he'll always be lionized for fighting for the

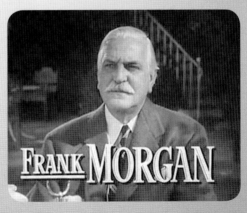

Frank Morgan / The White Cliffs of Dover *(trailer)*

unionization of his fellow actors in a guild that is thriving into a new century. Also, as important as the name "Morgan" was at MGM, the Barrymore family was THE dynasty on the lot. And, like so many impoverished artists and writers of the nineteenth century whose worth was appreciated only after death, Frank Morgan never lived long enough to see his most plum role remembered for generations.

The youngest in a family of eleven children, Morgan followed his older brother Ralph into acting, first on stage and then into the world of cinema. The elder Morgan had a bit of his brother's luck playing fourth fiddle to all three Barrymores (Lionel, Ethel, and John) in **Rasputin and the Empress**. He excelled as villains in small movies, and settled into a quiet, dignified career on television. Fortunately, Ralph played an important part in real-life Hollywood as one of the co-founders of the Screen Actors Guild. He was elected as the union's first president, and held the post twice in his career. SAG remains today the chief proponent of protection for actors in the United States in relationship with motion picture studio management. Ralph is fondly remembered for his initial courage in standing up to heads of studios, uniformly representing on-screen talent by proposing better wages and the need for health benefits.

Frank Morgan began his career in earnest during the Silent Era at Paramount Studios. After appearing in a few talkies in the early thirties supporting Fredric March, Ginger Rogers, Al Jolson, Harry Langdon, and Carole Lombard, he was noticed by Metro-Goldwyn-Mayer who lured him away. Despite his brother's off-screen battles, Frank Morgan had a wonderfully cordial relationship with Louis B. Mayer, the

MGM's Louis B. Mayer with his family at the White House

boss at MGM. In fact, he was so well thought of, Mayer gave him a lifetime contract. Of course, Lionel Barrymore was given the same option. It seemed Morgan was always a step behind Barrymore. Both actors, though friendly rivals, worked only once together in **Saratoga**. Barrymore was given billing behind Clark Gable and Jean Harlow (she died during the production of the film), but ahead of Morgan. Morgan was twice nominated for an Academy Award, the first time in 1934 for **The Affairs of Cellini**. By this time, Barrymore had already won an Oscar in 1931.

Frank Morgan really was wonderful in **The Great Ziegfeld** in 1936. In the movie, he portrays a fictional rival to the great impresario. William Powell as *Ziegfeld* steals his star act, *The Great Sandow*, setting their lifetime rivalry in motion. The film is a technically accurate depiction of *Ziegfeld*'s life, though the script takes many liberties with the timing of the facts. However, the motion picture took the top prize at the Academy Awards ceremony.

In 1939, the buzz around the studio lot was that an important picture was going into production soon. Many of MGM's actors wanted the opportunity to play a part in this movie. Director Ernst Lubitsch handled the script. Louis B. Mayer offered a choice role to Frank Morgan, but only if he appeared in another film. Morgan agreed to co-star in **The Wizard of Oz** just to be a part of **The Shop around the**

Florence Ziegfeld lithograph showcasing Sandow Trocadero

Director Ernst Lubitsch and his wife

Corner. He was assigned the role of *Mr. Matuschek*, the proprietor of a Hungarian store. Essentially it's a love story featuring James Stewart and Margaret Sullavan in the lead. Morgan sympathetically balances his assignment of fiercely maintaining the shop while his screen marriage deteriorates. Noted actor Joseph Schildkraut portrays the villain in the subplot that forces *Matuschek* to confront his own demons.

At the end of scheduled production, Morgan confidently predicted this was the part he'd be remembered for. There's no doubt *The Shop around the Corner* earned an important place in motion picture lore. In 1999, the National Film Registry selected the movie as one of its most important culturally significant works. MGM re-made it into a musical in 1949, re-titled *In the Good Old Summertime. You've Got Mail,* starring Tom Hanks and Meg Ryan, was a 1998 comedy remake of the classic film.

The absolute delight of *The Wizard of Oz*: L. Frank Baum's related stories were beloved by youngsters all over the world since the turn of the century. Morgan gladly honored his commitment to Louis B. Mayer. He was given the extraordinary task of playing five parts in the movie: "The

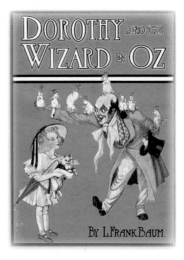

Dorothy and the Wizard of Oz *(1908 Cover)*

Wizard," *Professor Marvel*, a door attendant, a carriage driver, and a guard. He's at his blustery best in *Oz*. Master of the "aside" comment, many of his funniest lines in the movie occur during ad-libs thrown to the audience after he recited his portion of the script. His brand of comedy was copied to perfection by noted comedian Paul Ford, whose work on television's **Sgt. Bilko**, and later in **The Music Man** and **It's a Mad Mad Mad Mad World** exemplified the type of silliness Morgan proudly called his own decades earlier.

The Wizard of Oz (L. Frank Baum drawing)

Despite Mayer's assurance that **The Wizard of Oz** would receive a big budget, the schedule was a big headache by all who worked on the project. Fox Studios refused to lend Shirley Temple out to play the lead. Jack Haley replaced Buddy Ebsen as *The Tin Man* due to skin allergies from the paint dust used to cover his face. Noted actress Gale Sondergaard refused a part offered, leaving a relatively unknown Margaret Hamilton to play *The Wicked Witch of the West*. She suffered a muscular injury in a fall during her melting scene. The little folks who played *The Munchkins* were also an unruly bunch. And, Director Victor Fleming rushed the conclusion of *Oz* to get to **Gone with the Wind**, after Clark Gable had George Cukor fired from David O. Selznick's blockbuster film. Many in the former crew hoped the tornado that sent *Dorothy's* house soaring might destroy the set!

Frank Morgan/The Wizard of Oz *(trailer)*

One bit of irony regarding the film casting had to do with the actress who appeared as *Glinda, the Good Witch*. Billie Burke was the widow of Florence Ziegfeld. She became an ally to Morgan throughout the filming schedule since he had been a co-star in the production of **The Great Ziegfeld**. Myrna Loy portrayed Burke in a delightfully positive performance. Burke was forced to return to show business after the 1929 stock market crash wiped out Ziegfeld's fortune. She learned of his mishandling of funds only after he died. Burke was a

The Wonderful Wizard of Oz
(illustration)

gifted comedienne and shined playing ditzy wives including Roland Young's in **Topper Returns**, and Lionel Barrymore's (*ugh…*that name again!) in the all-star extravaganza **Dinner at Eight**.

Myrna Loy/The Great Ziegfeld *(trailer)*

The forties were a great decade for Morgan. He once again appeared with Clark Gable in **Boom Town** and **Honky Tonk**, with Mickey Rooney in **The Human Comedy**, with Gary Cooper in **Casanova Brown**, and he received an Oscar nomination playing a Mexican peasant in the film adaptation of John Steinbeck's classic, **Tortilla Flat**. Critics today regard this film as generally unimportant for a variety of reasons. The main complaint has to do with the casting of the movie. Spencer Tracy, Hedy Lamarr, John Garfield, and Morgan were top-notch actors in the MGM family, but hardly Latino. That said, the performances are dignified, if a trifle stereotypical. The story accurately depicts the closeness of poor villagers and their belief in God when all are working together for the same chance at happiness.

Frank Morgan/Tortilla Flat *(trailer)*

Alexandre Dumas was given an all-star treatment when MGM released **The Three Musketeers** in 1948. Morgan was offered the chance to perform as the *King of France* in a broadly comical role. Dumas couldn't have had Morgan in mind to play the chief steward of *The Musketeers*, but he handles himself well in a royal court mixed with gallantry and treachery.

In one of his final performances, Frank Morgan joined James Stewart and June Allyson in **The Stratton Story**. Monte Stratton was a Chicago White Sox pitcher whose career was cut short because of a hunting accident. Despite Stratton's leg amputation, he made a comeback (of sorts) in the minor leagues. Morgan is Stratton's manager, and the movie features real major league ballplayers including Bill Dickey and Jimmy Dykes. Much of the games were filmed at Comiskey Park in Chicago where Stratton actually played in the mid-thirties for the White Sox.

Frank Morgan suffered a fatal heart attack during the filming of **Annie Get Your Gun** in 1949 and had to be replaced. Louis Calhern assumed the role of *Buffalo Bill Cody*. Morgan's drinking problem likely attributed to his death. He was only 59.

Sadly, Morgan never saw **The Wizard of Oz** grow as a legendary motion picture. Television was in its infancy in 1949 and no one in show biz ever thought the movie would become a yearly event for folks of all ages. The small screen cemented the movie's place in celluloid history. An added bonus—the music composed by Harold Arlen and E. Y. Harburg—guaranteeing the film's life for decades to come. *"Bust my buttons…that's a horse of a different color!"* one of Morgan's characters surely might have exclaimed.

In 2009, MGM celebrated the 70th anniversary of *Oz* by re-releasing a DVD of this treasured piece of cinema, and included a new documentary with previously unreleased footage. A nationwide theater engagement of the motion picture in

Frank Morgan Tombstone,
Hollywood CA

high-definition also caused a magical stir by a new generation of viewers. There is little doubt that L. Frank Baum's creation will continue to delight well into the next century. And please, pay attention to the man behind the curtain near the end of the film. I can assure you it's not a Barrymore! Keep this in mind the next time you're off to see Frank Morgan, *"the wonderful Wizard of Oz."*

We're Off to See the Wizard
(lyric sheet)

MILWAUKEE'S FINEST

Jack Carson (1910-1963)

MILWAUKEE IS THE TWENTY-THIRD LARGEST CITY in the United States and home originally to a variety of Native Americans (mostly Sioux). German settlers inhabited the area by 1840 looking for a quieter way of life. Eventually, brewing and farming became the essential businesses that thrived in this community. Today, Milwaukee is known for its cold climate, and its independent spirit.

Milwaukee, WI *(circa 1890)*

The character actor versatile in light comedies, important dramas, and a number of musicals was a transplanted Canadian who grew up in Milwaukee. Jack Carson was a tall, relatively good-looking hunk, who had a knack for playing befuddled types to perfection. His amiable nature proved to be a tremendous asset as he accepted a variety of roles, no matter how small. And, a series of mishaps before he was discovered provided clouds with silver linings that led to a career filled with great performances in top-notch movies. Wisconsin's

Jack Carson/ Two Guys from Milwaukee (trailer)

favorite son proudly bragged of his Midwest upbringing, and in return, his hometown remained loyal to the actor throughout his life. The irony of this relationship…he never became a US citizen.

Carson intended to become a member of the Armed Services, attending St. John's Military Academy. At 6'2" and 220 lbs, he resembled the prototypical soldier. However, he decided to try acting while in college. He even garnered the lead in a stage production of **Hercules**. During one of the performances, Carson tripped off stage and took down the first couple of rows. A friend made him aware of his comedic ability, which led to his trying vaudeville as part of

Ginger Rogers

a team. They traversed the countryside and ended up in Hollywood. RKO discovered Carson and put him in a few films. His big break came in radio when Bing Crosby decided the bit-player was funny. Bing convinced the producers of **The Kraft Music Hall** to hire the comedian. Throughout his film career, Carson returned to radio and eventually hosted his own show beginning in 1943.

While at RKO, he frequently supported Ginger Rogers in small roles in **Stage Door**, **Vivacious Lady**, **Carefree**, and *Lucky Partners*. Sometimes uncredited, Carson still caught the attention of other studios and audiences. Universal borrowed the actor to reunite him with James Stewart (who starred in *Vivacious Lady*) in the comedic Western classic *Destry Rides Again*. Frank Capra also hired him to play a wisecracking

William Powell/Love Crazy *(trailer)*

reporter who acts as a compatriot to Thomas Mitchell in the landmark *Mr. Smith Goes to Washington* (again with Stewart).

The 1930s were a magical time for writers of comedy. "Screwball" became the nickname attributed to the style of fast-paced humor on film that was ridiculous in premise, and required incredible timing by actors trained in drama. William Powell, Cary Grant, Katharine Hepburn, and Carole Lombard succeeded in entering screwball comedies into the pantheon of great filmmaking. *Bringing up Baby* is a great example of the genre. Jack Carson's dopey persona and clumsy nature generated his career on a fast track to success. After appearing in a small role in the Grant / Hepburn vehicle, he followed with *Mr. and Mrs. Smith* and *Love Crazy*.

Early Warner Brothers logo

Warner Brothers was known for gritty dramas and gangster films. The studio searched for an actor who could play in their versions of screwball comedies. They signed Carson to a long contract in 1941. By this time, James Cagney grew tired of playing gangsters. To appease their box-office draw, Warner Brothers provided a few comedies for him to star in, surrounding the star with character actors who could churn out humorous scenes, such as in **The Strawberry Blonde** and **The Bride Came C.O.D.**—the latter featuring Eugene Pallette, William Frawley, George Tobias, and their newest find, Jack Carson, to support Cagney. Carson and Pallette also co-starred with Henry Fonda

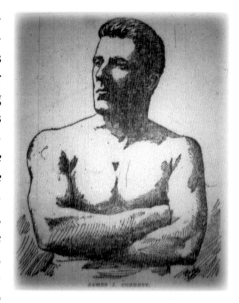

Boxer James J. Corbett

and Olivia de Havilland in **The Male Animal**. He also played Errol Flynn's best friend in **Gentleman Jim**, the lively biography of turn-of-the-century boxer James J. Corbett. Carson was typecast as the guy who loses the girl to Flynn.

He truly excelled in the 1941 motion picture **Arsenic and Old Lace** as a cop trying to win the attention of Cary Grant with a screenplay he has written. The problem with the movie lay in its

Jack Carson, Joan Crawford and Dennis Morgan/It's a Great Feeling (trailer)

delayed distribution, which was part of an agreement with the original Broadway show. By then, Carson had established himself as a strong supporting player. Critics were convinced this was a breakthrough role for the actor. Because of Warner Brothers' ironclad contract with the theatre production, he'd have to wait to catch the attention of his studio to put him in bigger parts.

Carson was also cast in a number of somber movies. He rose to each occasion, even if it meant appearing in just a few scenes. In **Blues of the Night**, he's a member of an ensemble jazz group. **The Hard Way** starred Ida Lupino in a film featuring Carson as husband to Joan Leslie, and an eventual suicide victim. After his celebrated success in **Arsenic and Old Lace**, the movie studio had him co-star as a conniving real estate agent in **Mildred Pierce**. Joan Crawford won an Oscar as Best Actress, but critics lauded Ann Blyth and Carson for their crackling, cynical performances in this melodramatic piece.

Warner Brothers rewarded the comedian by pairing him with Dennis Morgan in movies that were supposed to rival Bob Hope and Bing Crosby's *Road* pictures for Paramount. The actors actually appeared together previously in **Thank Your Lucky Stars** and **The Hard Way**. Though mildly popular, Morgan and Carson were never a threat to Hope and Crosby in terms of success with screen audiences. As in the *Road* films, one of the actors would get the girl; the other would get the

Bob Hope and Bing Crosby/Road to Bali *(trailer)*

laughs. The good-looking Morgan was the general beneficiary of this plot line. The one exception was **Two Guys from Milwaukee**, which actually had audiences rooting for Carson. He portrays a New York cabbie named *Buzz*, originally hailing from the land of dairy and beer. He reluctantly becomes famous after inadvertently delivering a nationwide radio message about the value of democracy over a monarchy (no matter how benevolent). The premise of a taxi driver ending up in this situation is fantastic, but Carson's speech rings true. This moment played well to postwar theatergoers.

One of the gals winning the scripted affection of Morgan was Doris Day. In reality, Jack Carson discovered Day, and they had an off-screen romance prior to his eventual marriage to Lola Albright. He appeared with Doris Day in several musical comedies. Ironically, Carson might be remembered best for starring in a low-budget film called **The Good Humor Man**. The part was written for Red Skelton, but Carson assumed the role at the last minute. It was an extremely popular flick. He continued to support in gentle comedies throughout the 1950s, including **Dangerous When Wet**, **Red Garters**, and **Phffft!**

Doris Day

Though he played in mostly likeable fair, Carson dabbled in drama. His finest roles: **A Star Is Born** with Judy Garland and James Mason, and **Cat on a Hot Tin Roof** starring Paul Newman, Elizabeth Taylor, and Burl Ives. In the latter film, he plays Newman's shrewish brother. Tennessee Williams wrote the stage play, and it was adapted to the screen by Richard Brooks. As in **Mildred Pierce**, the stars in each film received Oscar nods, while Carson received the best reviews of his career.

1920's Jewish Gambler
Arnold Rothstein

Carson is even credible in the marginal **King of the Roaring 20's**, a fictionalized account of 1920s Jewish gambling mogul Arnold Rothstein, played by David Janssen. In reality, he's considered the "*Moses of the modern Mafia*." Rothstein initiated the business blueprint demonstrating the profitability of Prohibition, and developed the concept of "organized crime." He was also the influential mastermind in the fixing of the 1919 World Series, known as "*The Black Sox Scandal*." Damon

Runyon glamorized his conceptual patronage of floating crap games in **Guys and Dolls**. The character *Nathan Detroit* was patterned after the gambler. His peers would dispose of Rothstein in 1928 for refusing to pay off gambling debts. His death contributed to the fall of Tammany Hall, and the political rise of Mayor Fiorello La Guardia.

Carson guest-starred on television frequently, including memorable appearances on **Bonanza** and **The Twilight Zone**, among others. He also hosted his own variety show. He decided in late 1962 to give Broadway a try. It just wasn't meant to be. He collapsed on stage during rehearsals of **The Critic's Choice**. Stomach cancer took him on January 2, 1963. Curiously, actor Dick Powell died the same day.

His career ended the same way it began…with a stumble. In between, Jack Carson made few pratfalls with regards to screen performances. He was likeable, and should be remembered as a shining beacon from Milwaukee during Hollywood's Golden Age.

Jack Carson/Mildred Pierce *(Trailer)*

Jack Carson (1910-1963)

Lon Chaney Jr

Peter Lorre

CHAPTER FOUR

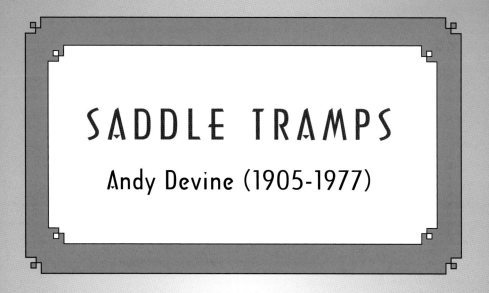

SADDLE TRAMPS

Andy Devine (1905-1977)

AMERICAN EDUCATOR HENRY WADSWORTH LONGFELLOW delivered the poetry that first suggested the idea of a "horse's tramp of hoofs" in his work *Paul Revere's Ride* in 1861. Revere was instrumental in a call to arms aboard the saddle of his trusty steed, which started the Revolutionary War. This story remains the reason the patriot's memory endures in our collective history.

In truth, Longfellow wrote his work to establish a national legend. The noted abolitionist wanted to promote a sense of urgency in the North about the South's potential secession. The poem is neither technically accurate, nor did it stop the advent of the Civil War. Revere didn't wait on his horse for the lantern

Paul Revere's Ride *(illustration)*

signal that sent him on his courageous jaunt. He hid in the Old North Church, and set the evening's actions in motion from there. He's also one of three riders who attempted to warn the Lexington townsfolk of an impending attack. And, the "*midnight ride*" actually took place over the course of three days. Revere never reached his destination because a British militia detained him. Despite these contradictions, a hero was born—all due to Henry Wadsworth Longfellow.

Henry Wadsworth Longfellow

The saddle tramp evolved as the name for drifters who wandered into neighboring towns in search of work and relaxation in the old West. They belonged to no collective and they didn't stay in one place for long. Outlaws and gunslingers might also hire these American nomads, driven to desperation for want of work. Often these early hobos rode in groups, fresh from a cattle drive, a roundup, or some other temporary job. Handling a team of horses from atop a stage, or as part of a posse, meant silver in their pocket for their effort. They spent their day's wages on drink, gambling, women, and a bath (or a shave). The saddle tramp wasn't a rancher, landowner, or businessman. However, he's a revered part of sagebrush lore.

The Cowboy *(circa 1888)*

As the Western genre became popular in movies and radio, a certain type was needed to play the dependable saddle tramp. These characters were relegated as friends of the lead, providing comic relief as part of the subplot. One of the first was Smiley Burnette, who traveled alongside Gene Autry. Primarily a songwriter, Burnette composed many of the melodies Autry sang in his movies. The star repaid his benefactor by suggesting to producers that he be cast as a cowpoke. Their union lasted through sixty movies in a twenty-year period. Burnette also joined Roy Rogers and Bob Livingston in the same capacity. His lingering legacy

Smiley Burnette/Phantom Empire
(trailer)

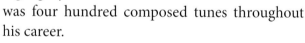

Gabby Hayes/Bad Man's Territory
(trailer)

was four hundred composed tunes throughout his career.

The most successful celluloid saddle bum was George "*Gabby*" Hayes, who first teamed with William Boyd in the **Hopalong Cassidy** series. Typecast for the rest of his career, Hayes even retained the rights to the names *Windy* and *Gabby*. He became a sidekick to Roy Rogers, Gene Autry (when Burnette was unavailable), Randolph Scott, and John Wayne. He also hosted his own television show in the fifties. Often found whittling wood and spouting off stories leading

William Boyd as
Hopalong Cassidy

Andy Devive (1905-1977)

into a particular sequence, Hayes seldom starred in the actual episode. Mel Brooks later paid tribute in **Blazing Saddles** by creating a character resembling the furry actor.

Along with the success of Roy, Gene, and *Hoppy*, the Western serial came into vogue in the mid-to-late thirties. Every radio, film, (and eventual television) cowboy had their companion by his side.

Texas Ranger (circa 1846 drawing)

The Cisco Kid relied on *Pancho,* primarily played by Louis Sorin and Leo Carrillo. **The Lone Ranger** traveled with *Tonto,* since Indians made ideal saddle tramps. Native Americans could only own land on reservations, and were often ridiculed by the White townsfolk. Victor Daniels was *Tonto* in a couple of film serials. John Todd portrayed *The Ranger's* faithful friend for much of the run on radio, while Jay Silverheels co-starred with Clayton Moore on television.

The Three Mesquiteers was a successful episodic vehicle for John Wayne, featuring Ray "*Crash*" Corrigan and Raymond Hatton in support. Other noted actors who participated in the series included Bob Livingston, Bob Steele, and Tom Tyler. Fifty-one episodes were produced over an eight-year period.

Guinn "*Big Boy*" Williams, Chill Wills, Pat Buttram, Harry Carey, Jr., Millard Mitchell, Jay C. Flippen, and Jack Elam portrayed other popular cinema tramps of the West. Walter Brennan and Ward Bond also occasionally played sagebrush buddies to John Wayne and James Stewart (among others).

Badge of a Texas Ranger

On radio, Joel McCrea starred in **Tales of the Texas Rangers**, a twentieth-century look at modern companions who often continued to fight crime with a distinct deference to our frontier past.

Despite the fame of Burnette and Hayes at the time, Andy Devine remains the most beloved individual to ride alongside the star of a motion picture. He wandered in and out of Westerns with a unique voice and a measure of talent. His high-pitched wheezy vocal patter was the result of a childhood accident. Of course, his delivery became his trademark. He could be funny, sentimental, and dramatic (frequently within the same movie). He was a cut above the other celluloid tramps who ever traveled on horseback. Devine also co-starred in other roles outside of Westerns, making him a versatile commodity in the process. Of course, movie studios were initially reluctant to hire him in talkies. John Ford took a chance on casting the actor in 1933, and his influential backing led to outstanding roles for the rotund actor in groundbreaking movies. Devine would eventually appear in over four hundred pictures.

Andy Devine was busy in the thirties co-starring in **Romeo and Juliet**, and the first screen production of **A Star Is Born**. John Ford noticed improvement in his work and decided he was the right actor to complement his cast in the 1939 production of **Stage-coach**.

Andy Devine/Man Crazy *(trailer)*

He portrayed *Buck*, the stage driver, with George Bancroft as the marshal joining him as his travel companion. Together, they maneuver the team through rough terrain in search of *The Ringo Kid*, and into the teeth of Apache-country. Ford is instrumental in broadening the importance of Westerns in cinema, and made a star of John Wayne. The director started emphasizing accuracy in locale, scripts, and characterizations to right the wrongs made by early filmmakers. Devine benefited from Ford's ideals.

He replaced Gabby Hayes in a number of movies that starred Roy Rogers. Devine became *Cookie* in these Saturday matinee releases. His roles in these films elevated the picture's popularity. Andy Devine was also a memorable featured sidekick in radio's **The Adventures of Wild Bill Hickok**. He reprised his character of *Jingles* in the movie and television versions. He became a semi-regular on **The Jack Benny Radio Program**, nicknaming the comedian *Buck* (an obvious reference to **Stagecoach**). Benny was flattered by this gesture. He developed a popular motion picture comedy, calling it **Buck Benny Rides Again.**

American novelist Stephen Crane

The Red Badge of Courage *(first edition cover)*

Arthur Hunnicutt/Split Second *(trailer)*

In 1951, World War II hero Audie Murphy starred in the film adapted from Stephen Crane's short story **The Red Badge of Courage**. To support Murphy in the Civil War drama, John Huston hired Devine, the fabulous Arthur Hunnicutt, and Royal Dano. The short story text was required reading in schools across the country, but the well-made film flopped at the box office. Huston always blamed MGM for its poor reception because of the way the movie was edited. Today, historians regard the motion picture as an essential work, which accurately depicts the ground confrontation during the War Between the States.

Interestingly, Commander James Harmon Ward (Devine's great-grandfather) became the first naval officer killed in the Civil War. Ward first saw action on June 1, 1861 as he commanded a flotilla, and was dead by June 27th. He traveled aboard the *Thomas Freeborn* on Chesapeake Bay and died from a fatal bullet to his abdomen.

Director William Wellman always tackled difficult stories throughout his career. A World War I pilot, he directed the first movie to win an Oscar—the landmark aviation film **Wings**. His crowning achievement was **The Ox-Bow Incident** in 1943. A decade later, Wellman developed **Island in the Sky**, chronicling the bravery of military survivors of a plane crash and the heroism displayed by fellow-airmen in search of the wreckage. Andy Devine, Lloyd Nolan, James Arness, and Paul Fix are the brave pilots who rescue the team. John Wayne plays the tough leader of survivors who brave an unfathomable temperature in order to stay alive. The locale was the rugged terrain in Quebec's

Commander James H. Ward, US Navy

Director William Wellman (as a 1919 flight instructor)

Island in the Sky (trailer)

uncharted territory. Devine is uncharacteristically heroic, and he received glowing reviews for his performance. Due to legal issues, the motion picture wasn't shown on television until 2005. For this reason, **Island in the Sky** is generally considered a lost gem.

While Westerns remained popular on television in the fifties, they were less so in cinema., Devine kept working, however, and even hosted a children's show on NBC. His signature voice was also used in cartoons and in commercials. He had cameo roles in **Around the World in Eighty Days,** playing the first mate on the USS Henrietta to Jack Oakie; and in **It's a Mad Mad Mad Mad World** appearing as a sheriff in a remote town in rural California.

John Ford called upon the durable actor to co-star as a comically frightened sheriff in **The Man Who Shot Liberty Valance**. Once again, Devine was teamed with John Wayne in a film that also features James Stewart, Lee Marvin, Edmond O'Brien, and Vera Miles. Devine was right at home with Walter Brennan and Pat O'Brien in **The Over-the-Hill Gang** in 1969. Other actors in the film included veteran tramps Chill Wills, Jack Elam, and Edgar Buchanan. Film-goers loved this comedic Western, so the producers created a sequel.

Andy Devine's last major role was in a Louisiana stage production of **Showboat**. He continued working until his death in 1973.

Henry Ford

The invention of the automobile signaled the end of primary travel by horse. When Henry Ford started mass-producing car seats, the romance of the saddle tramp would be remembered only in Hollywood. In December of 2009, The Roy Rogers and Dale Evans Museum in Branson, Missouri closed because of a nationwide economic downturn. The facility graciously offered *Trigger* (stuffed) to the Smithsonian Institution. Sadly, they were turned down due to a lack of space. Roy's descendants saw this decision as the official end of an era.

Andy Devine/Yellow Jack *(trailer)*

Andy Devine helped pave the way in motion pictures for television to honor the men who traveled our country on horseback. His career highlights can be enjoyed at the Mohave Museum of History and Arts in his hometown. Moreover, the main street of Kingman, Arizona was renamed *Andy Devine Avenue* in his honor. Dennis Weaver as *Chester Proudfoot* and Ken Curtis as *Festus* in **Gunsmoke** are two individuals (as well as others) who benefited from the work of Devine and his cohorts willing to ride alongside their companions in an effort to explore and tame our wilderness. Their natural curiosity and loyalty made America strong. We can be grateful the saddle tramp never took a back seat to anyone.

The Saddle Tramp

*Alan
Hale Sr.*

*Jack
Carson*

CHAPTER FIVE

PATHOS: THE CURSE OF A LIFETIME

Lon Chaney Jr. (1906-1973)

UNIVERSAL STUDIOS HAD A HAMMERLOCK on the horror genre during the studio era. Their stable of stars, directors and writers understood the very nature of putting the face on a memorable monster. An eerie remote locale…dark and desperate situations…flawed characters (including a fair share of assorted loathsome ghouls)…and a script tinged with wicked humor—this was the recipe for success.

These "B" pictures made household names of Bela Lugosi, Boris Karloff, Colin Clive, Claude Rains, Basil Rathbone, and Lionel Atwill. The supporting cast was just as remarkable. Dwight Frye, David Manners, Elsa Lanchester, Ernest Thesiger, Una O'Connor, and Director James Whale thrived in early thrillers. During the

Bela Lugosi

Lionel Atwill/Ghost of Frankenstein
(trailer)

British Actor Ernest Thesiger

forties, Evelyn Ankers, George Zucco, J. Carroll Naish, Glenn Strange, and John Carradine dabbled at the studio famous for fright.

Rains, Rathbone, and Carradine used the studio as a springboard toward "important" motion pictures. Lugosi supported a drug habit with his typecasting. Karloff, the amazingly prolific star of the horror flick, longed for the chance to do other types of roles. Many actors at Universal responded to imaginative screenplays with over-the-top performances. However, no actor embraced terror better than Lon Chaney Jr., employing a novel approach he learned from his famous father. His personal understanding of pathos, and his sincere application of its principle, made him a fruitful star of the scary movie. And maybe, the most underrated.

Chaney earnestly underplayed his scripted situations, concentrating on inner human frailties and the hidden resignation of potential victimization that cynically lie within us. Conversely, he also displayed total resolve where death could be the ultimate result with conviction of purpose. Moviegoers

Lon Chaney Jr./House of
Frankenstein (trailer)

alternately rooted for his success and his demise. Chaney became Hollywood's first cinematic anti-hero during its Golden Age. He embraced his assignments, improving with each opportunity. The next generation of ghoulish actors, including Vincent Price and Christopher Lee (plus Jonathan Frid as vampire *Barnabas Collins* in television's **Dark Shadows**), imitated his technique with varying degrees of success. Consequently, Lon Chaney Jr. secured the genre's popularity into the new century. And he became a consummate actor, earning the respect of his peers that stretched over his entire career.

Christopher Lee/Horror Hotel *(trailer)*

Named Creighton at birth, he was the firstborn to silent screen star Lon Chaney. The elder Chaney was the melodramatic counterpart to Charlie Chaplin, Buster Keaton, Rudolph Valentino, Gloria Swanson, and Mary Pickford. He became a superstar of the silent era. Lon Sr. applied his craft well because of his pinpoint ability to pantomime. He developed his expertise of visual expression while growing up with parents who were both deaf. He also learned how to handle ridicule that comes with affliction.

Lon Chaney Sr./The Miracle Man *(still)*

A loving child, Chaney empathized with his folks' condition and protected them throughout their lives. Even in marriage, he endured a first wife who irrationally feared for her child's well-being. The early twentieth century was a time when the public incorrectly surmised that hearing deficiencies might be physically inherited. This concept drove Chaney's partner to a suicide attempt. Their union dissolved over the matter.

As a result, Lon Chaney created memorably tormented silent screen characters. The use of makeup and contortionism cemented his propensity for grabbing at the heartstrings of audiences worldwide. Affectionately regarded as *The Man of a Thousand Faces*, he actively searched for roles appealing to the misunderstood. The term "monster" was used to describe his parts in **The Hunchback of Notre Dame** and **The Phantom of the Opera**. He eventually re-married and managed to keep his son out of acting. Unfortunately, Chaney died of cancer in 1930 after making the only talkie in his career.

Lon Chaney Sr./The Phantom of the Opera (still)

Creighton learned life lessons on how to relate to individuals different from the norm. After his father's death, he adapted the elder Chaney's acting style. Pathos ticketed his appeal with filmgoers. Unlike tragedy, which results from the purposeful and at times malicious intent of a given action, pathos is the unintentionally creative and imaginative sadness stirred to help us understand unemotional plights placed on innocent individuals. The younger Chaney understood the premise that unremarkable people could deliver abundant doses of pathos. He witnessed examples of this within his family and while working outside of Hollywood.

Because of his father's insistence, Creighton virtually had no experience in cinema. He owned the Chaney name—his eventual ticket into studio work—and learned his craft from the bottom up. He accepted whatever meager roles assigned, and started getting steady parts once he shrewdly changed his name to Lon Chaney Jr. His first success came in motion picture serials based on weekly radio programs and daily comic strips. Fortunately, dramatic serials are prime fodder for the dispensation of pathos, since recurring characters might endure a litany of problems in order to exist. Chaney honed his skills in early episodic flicks including **Undersea Kingdom**, Dashiell Hammett's **Secret Agent X-9**, and **Ace Drummond** (based on a comic strip created by American World War I ace Eddie Rickenbacker). He also appeared in *Mr. Moto* and *Charlie Chan* crime serials that starred Peter Lorre, Warner Oland, and Keye Luke.

Captain Eddie Rickenbacker, World War I ace

Because of his height (6'2") and large build, Chaney was cast in Westerns, usually as the henchman of a villain. By all accounts, he felt the genre would be his calling, since they were popular and easy to produce. Movie storylines were quite similar in early tales of the West. He appeared in over a dozen films during the thirties including **Jesse James**, **Union Pacific**, **Billy the Kid**, and **Northwest Mounted Police**. Although he returned to the Western in the fifties, two things worked against Lon Chaney Jr. in his favored career path. First, his studio home was Universal, best known for their horror films. Second, Chaney developed into a vastly talented actor and was constantly loaned to other studios. One role in particular molded the rest of career.

Chaney could have garnered an Oscar nomination for his performance as *Lennie Small* in John Steinbeck's **Of Mice and Men** had the movie not been released in that magical year of 1939. Nevertheless, this was a *tour de force* for the actor. Chaney received critical acclaim for his kind, dim- witted, and unintentionally dangerous portrayal. He also worked well with Burgess Meredith and the rest of the United Artists cast. Pathos is on full display in the Steinbeck adaptation and Chaney delivers it in spades. *Of Mice and Men* (the motion picture) remains the novelist's most eerily remembered work. Hal Roach Jr. of United Artists then parlayed the success of this motion picture by using the actor in *One Million B.C.* Chaney co-starred as a Cro-Magnon leader of a prehistoric tribe; a fantastic premise considering dinosaurs

John Steinbeck

became extinct long before the arrival of human life by all scientific accounts. However, movie audiences ate up the action and special effects despite the bona fide inaccuracy of the suggestion.

Universal Studios confidently found their successor to Boris Karloff, Claude Rains, and Bela Lugosi. Lon Chaney Jr. was immediately cast in *Man Made Monster* and in his signature role as *The Wolf Man*. He obliged with terrific performances. The irony of the latter movie comes from how the title character is victimized dur-

Lycaon changed into a wolf *(illustration)*

ing an act of heroism. In the chapter on Claude Rains in my first edition of *Forgotten Hollywood Forgotten History*, I explain the curse of the lycanthrope with its roots in Eastern European lore during The Middle Ages. What is stated with prominence in the script: "*Even a* man, who is pure in heart and says his prayers at night, may become a wolf when the wolf bane blooms and the autumn moon is full and bright." Lawrence Talbot (Chaney's character) loathed his situation, especially at the onset of the cyclical full moon causing his transformation. And his consequential grief after the fact was immense. Like a disease, lycanthropy lingered and endured to *Talbot's* chagrin. Chaney successfully developed this character helping him step from his father's formidable shadow. The elder Chaney might have been giddy with his son's coming-of-age by his effective use of pathos.

The Wolf Man *(trailer)*

The werewolf lives in the shadow of Bram Stoker and Mary Shelley's creations. Yet, Chaney's *Wolf Man* was unlike any fiend on Universal's lot. *Dracula* lustily enjoyed afterlife as a vampire in search of victims. A scientist created the *Frankenstein* monster with the accidental inclusion of a criminal's brain. Revenge on the local townspeople is malevolently exacted after his persecution. The *Invisible Man* injected his insanity with a foreign serum. *Dr. Jekyll* did the same thing. The *Mummy* suggested the pre-meditated promise of a grisly death to trespassers who desecrate his burial grounds. Tampering with God's law meant certain doom. The *Wolf Man* was not the consequence

Author Bram Stoker

Boris Karloff/Bride of Frankenstein *(trailer)*

of an experiment, or defiance to religion.

An added bonus was the addition of Maria Ouspenskaya in the film (and in **Frankenstein Meets the Wolf Man**). The diminutive gypsy, and mother to a werewolf, convincingly worked with *Talbot* in searching for a cure from his curse. Bela Lugosi played her blood son that placed this situation upon our hero. Ouspenskaya offered sober guilt for her role in his plight. Only the gypsy contained his beast within. The motion picture studio had a bona fide star for their "B" movie thrillers to replace Lugosi, who was rapidly falling into drug dependency.

Maria Ouspenskaya/Waterloo Bridge (trailer)

House of Frankenstein *(trailor)*

Unlike Boris Karloff, Lon Chaney Jr. gleefully accepted his work and managed to portray the *Wolf Man*, *Mummy*, *Dracula*, and even *Frankenstein* over the next decade. He was a love-interest to Evelyn Ankers and others. And he sought friendship from characters played by Ralph Bellamy, Patrick Knowles, Abbott and Costello, etc. However, when Chaney turned into a werewolf (for example),

Evelyn Ankers

he wanted to rip them all to shreds. His monsters were vicious, but he evenly displayed their humanity, and reasoned their victimization on screen. This was quite an impressive feat considering the predictably pedestrian nature of the scripts. He truly frightened theatergoers at a time when scary movies caused us at times to laugh out loud. For example, Colin Clive is genuinely funny in **Frankenstein** when he remarks about his monster, "*it's alive, it's alive.*" And Dwight Frye is alternately creepy and silly when searching for the juice of insects in **Dracula**. Chaney insisted the unearthly fiends in **Abbott and Costello Meet Frankenstein** play it straight to achieve a believable dichotomy. This savvy suggestion makes the film a combined comedy and horror classic. Only an amiable nature kept Lon Chaney Jr. from striving to become a true horror icon. Fans would fight the intelligent actor on this point.

Director Stanley Kramer was a huge fan of Chaney's work and decided to employ the actor whenever possible. In fact, Kramer's stated favorites in cinema were Spencer Tracy and Chaney. High praise from a producer who worked with Gary Cooper, Burt Lancaster, Gregory Peck, Katharine Hepburn, Gene Kelly, Judy Garland, Fredric March, Richard Widmark, Fred Astaire, Ava Gardner, Montgomery Clift, Theodore Bikel, Mickey Rooney, and Marlene Dietrich.

Stanley Kramer/Inherit the Wind *(trailer)*

Lon Chaney Jr/High Noon *(trailer)*

Lon Chaney Jr. (1906-1973)

Kramer hired Chaney to play a retired sheriff in **High Noon**. In the picture, he explains to the marshal (Cooper) why he would hinder his efforts to battle bad guys, all because of his advanced arthritis. It's a compelling scene from a skilled actor in a movie that featured Grace Kelly (in her second role), Katy Jurado, Thomas Mitchell, Lloyd Bridges, and Harry Morgan. Kramer also offered choice roles to Chaney in **Not as a Stranger** with Robert Mitchum, and in **The Defiant Ones** with Tony Curtis and Sidney Poitier.

As Lon Chaney Jr. matured, he wanted a chance to appear in different genres. Interspersed with horror flicks, such as **Bride of the Gorilla** and **Indestructible Man**, he eventually returned to Westerns, usually as an aging and ineffectual sheriff. He also portrayed a character similar to his *Lennie* in **My Favorite Brunette**, a Bob Hope vehicle. Chaney as *Frankenstein* treated a live television audience to a rousing performance in the anthology series **Tales of Tomorrow**. He also reprised his role as the *Wolf Man* one last time in an episode of **Route 66**. Unfortunately, major motion picture production companies stopped hiring him once he started heavily drinking. He traveled to Mexico to appear in low-budget creepers like RKO's **The Cyclops** in 1957. Despite the fact these films were cheaply made, Chaney was actually quite effective in them.

Though his unique brand of pathos was Lon Chaney Jr.'s strong suit, and while he battled alcoholism, no one ever accused him of living a pathetic life. He accepted being his father's son, the notion of studio system type-casting, and a gradual decline into minor character roles with grace, dignity, and professionalism. Chaney managed to deliver chilling performances on his own terms.

Lon Chaney Jr./Abbott and Costello Meet Frankenstein *(trailer)*

Since his death, his family has continually worked at keeping his image alive. His grandson continues to campaign to get a star for Chaney on *Hollywood's Walk of Fame*. And in 1997, the US Postal Service honored the *Wolf Man* in stamps commemorating cinematic monsters. Universal Studios recently released a remake of his signature movie with Benicio del Toro as *Lawrence Talbot*, Anthony Hopkins as his father, and Geraldine Chaplin as the gypsy. The Hispanic actor is an avid fan of the original film and a noted collector of *Wolf Man* memorabilia. In addition, a new film version of **Dark Shadows,** written and directed by Tim Burton, and with Johnny Depp as *Barnabas Collins* (a *Talbot*-esque character), as of this writing is in current development.

Like Walter Brennan, the mere mention of Lon Chaney Jr. evokes a provocative canvas of great screen roles, no matter how small the motion picture. I believe he might be proud of this unexpected accomplishment, a natural by-product of his disciplined effort at becoming a fine and respected actor who vastly appreciated the human condition. There's little doubt Chaney has finally achieved an iconic status that eluded him in life.

Katy Jurado

Gilbert Roland

CHAPTER SIX

A WANDERING STAR

S. Z. Sakall (1883-1955)

WHILE THE NAZIS INVADED EASTERN EUROPE during the German military doctrine of *Blitzkrieg* that initiated World War II, a whole host of creative elite (most of whom were Jewish) left their native countries. Remaining home meant boycott, ridicule, persecution, imprisonment, and certain death. Thousands of Germans, Austrians, Czechs, and Scandinavians made their way out of Hitler's path and his mad quest for the eradication of Jews, Bolsheviks, Catholics, gypsies, homosexuals, and others deemed inferior.

One positive consequence of this mass exodus was the talent now available to Hollywood in the form of writers, directors, and actors. American cinema could now stray from provincial tales to tell global stories with actual artisans from across the Atlantic. A great example

S.Z. Sakall/Small Town Girl
(trailer)

of the cosmopolitan performer suddenly looking for work in the United States arrived in the form of a rotund jovial Hungarian named S.Z. Sakall.

After earning success in Budapest vaudeville shows, Sakall traveled to Vienna and Berlin. He appeared in light romantic comedies that were popular during the silent era. His reputation grew and he decided to form his own film company, confident his career was set. When he turned fifty, the idea of retiring after a slew of successful productions became a plausible notion. The politics of the day rudely changed his plans. His first decision was to return to his native Hungary, where he made forty more movies. However, the Axis regime clearly wanted to expand their autocratic control in an uncompromising fashion. Sakall made the heartfelt choice to leave Europe for good in 1939 with the help of Producer Joseph Pasternak, a distant cousin, to test his talent in Hollywood. Sadly, many of his close relatives died in concentration camps as part of Hitler's *Final Solution,* including all three of his sisters, his niece, and his wife's siblings.

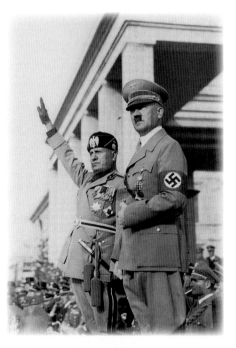

Adolph Hitler and Benito Mussolini in Italy

His transition was effortless. Sakall nurtured his ability in light romantic motion pictures to perfection. It also didn't hurt he was bilingual, speaking English most of his adult life. Film studios found a talented type to play European nobility, uncles, impresarios, or excitable shopkeepers. His accent helped when displaying intelligence as a professor or educator. Einstein's celebrity had reached our country, so it wasn't a stretch to assume Europeans were smart, resourceful, and innovative. An added bonus—S.Z. Sakall had a kind, friendly face. A human teddy bear, he inherited the moniker "*Cuddles*" early in his second career; a name he actually disliked. Needless to say, he was an instant success and memorable in all of his films.

Sakall was fortuitously cast in movie classics of the 1940s. Beginning with **The Devil and Miss Jones**, he had an unparalleled string of strong performances. Universal, RKO, and Fox Studios were eager to find roles for their comedic find. He joined an ensemble of storied character actors including Henry Travers in **Ball of Fire**, supporting Gary Cooper and Barbara Stanwyck. Both of these films received attention from the Academy of Motion Picture Arts and Sciences. His next two projects were blockbusters…and Oscar winners.

Gary Cooper and Barbara Stanwyck/
Ball of Fire *(trailer)*

Sakall's hatred of fascism prompted an enthusiastic performance in **Yankee Doodle Dandy**, the film that earned James Cagney an Academy Award. Sakall's blustery persona was on full display in this rousing patriotic musical. His comedic timing brought out the best in Cagney, Cooper, Stanwyck, and Humphrey Bogart.

Warner Brothers, Sakall's new studio home, immediately cast him in **Casablanca**. In this piece of cinematic perfection, he received the role of *Karl*, the head waiter at *Rick's Café American*. He's steadfastly loyal, gentle, and

James Cagney/Yankee Doodle
Dandy *(trailer)*

sympathetic to the *Resistance* against Nazi aggression in Northern Africa. Despite a lower billing, Sakall is given more screen time than either Sydney Greenstreet or fellow Hungarian Peter Lorre. The ensemble cast could be proud for the Oscar it garnered as the Best Picture of 1943. A Bogart cameo in **Thank Your Lucky Stars** features an uncharacteristically bold Sakall. He stands down the noted tough guy in an amusing bit, playing off Bogie's screen image.

Sakall's next role as a butcher might have been his finest, if not his most remembered. In **Wonder Man**, his scenes with Danny Kaye are priceless. The comedian was known for his musical tongue twisters, and his frenetic acting pace. Kaye was Samuel Goldwyn's golden boy, and his pairing with Virginia Mayo created sparks. The couple worked together in four projects. Ironically, Goldwyn remade **Ball of Fire** in

S.Z. Sakall and Humphrey Bogart/ Thank Your Lucky Stars *(trailer)*

Danny Kaye (during USO tour)

Virginia Mayo/The Best Years of our Lives *(trailer)*

1950 with the new title *A Song is Born*. The film did include Kaye and Mayo. However, Sakall was not hired to co-star in the picture (frankly this decision was a mistake).

Sakall was reunited with Stanwyck and Sydney Greenstreet in **Christmas in Connecticut** in 1945. The movie is generally regarded as a lost holiday classic. The **Turner Classic Movies Channel** was feverish in its promotion of this gem during their December look at Christmas in 2009.

Sakall showed his versatility as an actor when paired with Errol Flynn in **San Antonio**. Westerns were not a strong suit for the actor, but he was a welcome addition to this minor Flynn vehicle. He played a traveling elixir salesman in a part that would have been better suited for Alan Hale Sr.

The postwar era was a busy time for the comedian. He rejoined Errol Flynn in **Never Say Goodbye**, and co-starred with Jack Carson and Dennis Morgan in **Two Guys from Milwaukee**. Bogart and Lauren Bacall had an interesting comedic cameo at the conclusion of the latter movie. Sakall found the last scene rather amusing and is seen candidly laughing in the background, something the director didn't mind keeping in the final cut of the film. Sakall also appeared with Carson's close friend (shall we say) Doris Day in three motion pictures—**Romance on the High Seas**, **Tea for Two**, and **Lullaby of Broadway**. Day remained a lasting pal with the cuddly actor.

S.Z. Sakall/Two Guys from Milwaukee
(trailer)

Sakall secured a part in the remake of **The Shop around the Corner**. He inherited the Frank Morgan role of *Mr. Matuchek*, though his name and the title of the film were changed. **In the Good Old Summertime** was a natural opportunity for the actor, since the original took place in his native Budapest;

however, the locale was moved inexplicably to Chicago. The movie starred Judy Garland and Van Johnson. Garland's daughter, Liza Minnelli, made her acting debut at the tender age of three in this production. Interestingly, Buster Keaton marked his official comeback with a small part in the movie. He also co-directed some of the scenes, though he didn't receive screen credit for his off-screen work.

Buster Keaton

In 1951, Metro-Goldwyn-Mayer wanted to show off its stable of stars in an eight-part episodic feature called **It's a Big Country**. Essentially a docudrama, the epic starred Gary Cooper, Gene Kelly, Fredric March, Ethel Barrymore, William Powell, Van Johnson, Janet Leigh, Keenan Wynn, James Whitmore, Marjorie Main, and of course, S.Z. Sakall. Seven noted directors were used in the production including John Sturges, William Wellman, and Clarence Brown. MGM chief executive Dore Schary spent much of his time promoting his large cast. Some of the segments were clearly better than others, and the motion picture generally has an uneven quality.

Mario Lanza/That Midnight Kiss (trailer)

Sakall's final film was **The Student Prince**. The noteworthy reason for even mentioning this small film was its use of Mario Lanza's voice, though he didn't appear in the actual movie. Contractually, his singing was appropriated by MGM despite a dispute between the tenor and the studio. His

Hungarian Royal Palace in Budapest

vocal performance receives screen credit. For Sakall, this finale returned the actor to a scripted locale near Germany and Austria, though the actual kingdom is fictional. The setting takes place at the turn of the twentieth century.

S.Z. "Cuddles" Sakall never lived long enough to see his beloved Hungary free from despotic control, though he kept his citizenship papers on the mantel in his living room for the rest of his life. The Soviet tyranny of Stalin replaced Nazi occupation. Oppressive war (even a *Cold* one) became the misery of his life.

Soviet tanks and infantry attacking the German army near Budapest in 1944

The Siege of Budapest

S.Z. Sakall application for US citizenship

S. Z. Sakall (1883-1955)

Our good fortune is this soft-spoken talent found freedom in the United States. Because of his livelihood, this reluctant wanderer thrived and prospered until the day he died.

S.Z. Sakall/Small Town Girl *(trailer)*

CHAPTER SEVEN

CHILDREN OF THE DEPRESSION

THE POPULARITY OF MOTION PICTURES during the silent era grew as a national public clamored for their new-found medium of entertainment. Movie studios were quickly established by entrepreneurs willing to take a chance on making millions of dollars with this new creation of escapism. Mack Sennett, Hal Roach, and the United Artists team of D.W. Griffith, Charlie Chaplin, Douglas Fairbanks, and Mary Pickford succeeded in putting out quality product. All of their efforts came at a huge price, since few rules were put in place to protect talent. No unions existed at the time representing actors. Working by the day was a common practice. And if one signed a contract, individuals were at the mercy of their studio. Frankly, this occurred in all walks of business.

Upton Sinclair

Writer Upton Sinclair provided the first glimpse of unsanitary working conditions, and what he called *"wage-slavery"* within the meat packing industry in his novel **The Jungle** in 1906. Sinclair's novel prompted governmental examination of general exploitation. President Theodore Roosevelt tackled this issue with federal protection of labor, and he ordered the creation of laws to make plants nationwide more sanitary.

Meat inspection
(Swift & Co., Chicago)

Children in motion pictures were particularly susceptible to the whims of their parents and employers in the growing film industry. Movie studios might be subject to eventual federal overview, but a family living off the work of their youngsters was considered a private issue. One of the most famous casualties in this matter was Jackie Coogan, Charlie Chaplin's co-star in **The Kid**. Coogan's father, Jack Sr., was a former actor who saw his son's obvious talent for

Charlie Chaplin and Jackie Coogan/
The Kid (still)

mimicry. He protected the child and became his manager. However, Jack Sr. died in an auto accident in 1935, contractually leaving his son to provide for his mother and new stepfather. His net worth by 1938 rose to an estimated four million dollars, yet his family carelessly spent almost all of his savings. Coogan decided to sue his parents and won. He received about $126,000 after legal fees. Charlie Chaplin graciously offered financial support to Jackie during his leanest years. California promptly enacted *The Child Actor's Bill* (known as *The Coogan Act*), which protected all future working youngsters from parental encroachment. The growth of the Screen Actors Guild also offered insulation to all actors when talkies emerged.

Shirley Temple, Mickey Rooney, Judy Garland, and Jane Withers became immensely successful, and top box-office draws into adoles-

Jackie Coogan

cence. Few kids, however, had their talent, the luck necessary to enter the motion picture industry, or the standing to influence society. When the Stock Market crashed in 1929, going to school became a luxury for children across this country. Youngsters searched for real opportunities to help provide their own family with food and shelter. Earnest screenwriters wanted to mirror the

plight of America in their scripts. Like *The Kid* a decade earlier, children of the Depression (on film) needed to be streetwise, resourceful, and at times, morally compromised.

Eleanor Roosevelt and Shirley Temple

Carl "Alfalfa" Switzer (1927-1959)

The ***Our Gang*** series was the brainchild of Producer Hal Roach in 1921. These two-reel comedies pioneered the way theatre audiences saw children on screen. As the troupe aged, Roach replaced his cast with sensational kids who had a way of comically mirroring society. He also was color-blind in his casting of race and gender in important roles, emphasizing equality within the given cinematic neighborhood. For example, Ernie Morrison became the first person of color to receive a binding Hollywood contract, something Roach insisted upon.

During the Depression era of film, *The Little Rascals* became Midwest street urchins from suburban families in a variety of plot subtexts, recognizing modest values over entitlement while growing up. And, the children almost always solved their own scripted problems. Several of the cast also achieved unparalleled stardom while performing for Roach. Jackie Cooper and George "*Spanky*" McFarland became bona fide stars of the series.

Jackie Cooper/Broadway to Hollywood *(trailer)*

Cooper developed into a fine adult actor, while *Spanky* starred in over ninety shorts during a ten-year career. Both actors are recognized on *Hollywood's Walk of Fame*. Other tots most associated with the ***Our Gang*** series during this time include *Stymie* Beard, Darla Hood, *Buckwheat* Thomas, *Porky* Lee, *Froggy* Laughlin, and Mickey Gubitosi (later known as Robert Blake).

Spanky, Darla and Alfalfa/Our Gang Follies of 1938 *(still)*

Despite the success of Cooper and McFarland, the story of Carl "*Alfalfa*" Switzer was the most complex and tragic. *Spanky's* second fiddle may have been the finest comedian within the Roach ensemble of revolving actors. *Alfalfa* was fearless in showing what children across the country emoted—very human faults. He sang off-key, had a silly cowlick on the top of his head, and concocted harebrained schemes that got other children in trouble. Behind the scenes, he also had a knack for scaring his peers. His practical jokes were often cruel and painful. He carried pocket-knives and fish hooks in his pockets, which he used in tricks that caused purposeful injury. When Hal Roach sold the **Our Gang** series to MGM in 1938, Switzer became intolerable on sets. His father was also mindfully aggressive in negotiating contracts with mogul Louis B. Mayer.

His screen family was dissolved in 1940 when the series was terminated. Only twelve, Switzer attempted to maintain a solo career. He was marginally busy, appearing in a variety of engaging films including **The Human Comedy**, **Going My Way**, **The Courage of Lassie**, **It's a Wonderful Life** (as a young suitor to Donna Reed), **State of the Union**, and **Island in the Sky**. He reprised *Alfalfa* in the **Gas House Kids** comedies of the mid-1940s. He had a minor role in **The Defiant Ones**, and his photo was used in **White Christmas**. Rosemary Clooney and Vera Ellen refer to Switzer as their brother, and a former army pal to Bing Crosby and Danny Kaye in an amusing scene. Ironically, Hollywood discovered a way to contain the disruptive star.

During the 1950s, Carl Switzer started breeding hunting dogs. His clients included James Stewart, and Roy Rogers and Dale Evans (the couple were his godparents). He started committing minor crimes and often got in trouble with the law. In 1959, he confronted a hunting dog client at his home over a fifty-dollar debt owed Switzer. It's unclear what exactly happened after that, but, he did receive a gunshot wound to his stomach, which killed the thirty-one-year-old actor.

Leo Gorcey (1917-1969)

The most shocking disparity of wealth within this country during the Depression existed in our biggest cities. Particularly in New York and Chicago, tenement slums were built next to neighboring streets where the rich and opulent lived. At the corner of 53rd Street and the East River in Manhattan is a cul-de-sac, which during the 1930s was well-known for its crowded, unsanitary living conditions. Playwright Sidney Kingsley highlighted this destitute area in a dramatic Broadway production in 1935. Lillian Hellman adapted a screenplay for a film made two years later. *Dead End* provided a vivid glimpse of the working poor and unemployed who lived in large urban centers. At the heart of both productions were young actors, reminding audiences about the peril of growing up without hope. Crime provided an attractive and superficial solution. The film made instant stars of the ensemble dubbed *The Dead End Kids*.

The Dead End Kids/Angels with Dirty Faces
(trailer)

The Broadway version employed fourteen adolescents who played members of the gang and other children. The standouts in the theatre production were Billy Halop, Huntz Hall, Bobby Jordan, Bernard Punsly, Gabriel Dell, and Leo Gorcey. Actually, before the opening, Gorcey wasn't even in the original cast, though his younger brother David had a role. Leo only decided to give acting a try after he was fired as a plumber's apprentice. Unemployed, he spent his days watching rehearsals, which led to an understudy audition. Their father, Bernard, was successful in vaudeville, and mentored his two sons on how to obtain roles on stage.

When Producer Samuel Goldwyn and Director William Wyler were unsuccessful in their search for young actors to play the *Dead End Kids* on screen, they turned to the original Broadway drama. The six teens were superior in their tryouts. Each was given a two-year contract to appear in Hollywood films, beginning with the adapted screenplay of **Dead End**. Billy Halop had the movie star good looks to receive top billing among the ensemble. The other five actors supported Halop in a series of gangster pictures including **Crime School**, **Angels with Dirty Faces**, **They Made Me a Criminal**, and **Hell's Kitchen**. They co-starred with Humphrey Bogart, James Cagney, Pat O'Brien, Ann Sheridan, John Garfield, and Ronald Reagan (the top actors on the Warner Brothers lot). Halop showed little desire to remain with the gang beyond his contract. After serving in the military during World War II, he struggled to succeed in a subsequent solo career. By 1947, he was effectively out of show business.

Curiously, audiences started responding to Leo Gorcey. He created much of the drama within the plot, either by displaying false bravado, disloyalty, or cowardly behavior. He could also take a screen slap. Gorcey even appeared with his father in a movie or two including **Out of the Fog**. The 1941 motion picture featured Garfield, Ida Lupino, and Thomas Mitchell. It was

Leo Gorcey/Gallant Sons *(trailer)*

an early *film noir* examination of how everyday folks dealt with criminal extortion.

The young performers proved to be an unruly bunch, causing an acrimonious end with the studio once their contracts expired. Gorcey, Bobby Jordan, Huntz Hall, and Gabe Dell were given the chance to re-create their roles for Monogram Pictures as *The East*

Side Kids for twenty-one films, and subsequently, in a thirteen-year run as *The Bowery Boys*. These movies lacked the weight of the earlier productions in terms of budget and plot. They did become popular Saturday matinee comedies lasting well into the late 1950s. *The Bowery Boys* mimicked much of the slapstick comedy of Abbott and Costello, and the physical humor of The Three Stooges. Gone was

Huntz Hall/They Made Me a Criminal (trailer)

the emphasis on slum dwelling and serious overtones in plot. Audiences of postwar America showed no desire to be reminded about the Depression, since our nation's domestic effort against Nazi aggression reaped a healthy rebound to our economy.

Gorcey (as *Slip Mahoney)* and Hall (as *Sach Jones*) developed a great working relationship, forcing Jordan into the background and eventual retirement. Though well into his thirties, Leo Gorcey stood 5'6" tall, which helped him look youthful. Moreover, all he had to do was take his fedora and push the brim up and *voilá*…his trademark juvenile look.

Gorcey understood the fickle nature of theatergoers and protected his livelihood by suggesting they hire his father and brother for

Hollywood Walk of Fame Star of The Dead End Kids

many of these films. He also oversaw all decisions regarding how the movies were written. After forty-one popular *Bowery Boys* pictures, he retired from the series when his dad was killed in a car accident. His brother David replaced Leo in its final years.

He re-emerged in a cameo role as a cab driver in **It's a Mad Mad Mad Mad World** in 1963. Gorcey spent his last years writing his memoirs and drinking heavily. David eventually became a minister, counseled his brother, and protected him from actively damaging his reputation. Due to his brother's efforts, Leo Gorcey was rewarded with eternal youth in our collective cinematic memory.

Freddie Bartholomew (1924-1992)

Freddie Bartholomew was a huge child star during the advent of Hollywood's Golden Age. He rivaled Shirley Temple and Mickey Rooney in terms of popularity. Yet, his career was brief and he primarily appeared in period pieces. Unlike his contemporaries, he was an authentic character actor who spoke the words of top authors from the previous century.

Born in London, Bartholomew's parents abandoned him, leaving his aunt to raise him. He was three when he first appeared on the British stage. Producer David O. Selznick discovered the intelligent child with good looks while the family was on holiday in Hollywood. MGM cast him in the film adaptation of Charles Dickens' **David Copperfield,** which starred W. C. Fields and Lionel Barrymore. Fields famously claimed he hated

Freddie Bartholomew/Anna Karenina (trailer)

working with children and animals because of Bartholomew's scene-stealing ability. The movie received a nomination for Best Picture by the Motion Picture Academy in 1935.

The child's next appearance in *Anna Karenina* with Greta Garbo cemented a path to stardom for Bartholomew. The film was ambitiously adapted from a Leo Tolstoy novel. Today, the author is generally regarded as the greatest Eastern European writer of the nineteenth century. Tolstoy vividly captured the noble culture of his people, and *War and Peace* is considered his masterpiece. Unfortunately, he died in 1910, before the Russian peasantry knew much about their bard.

Leo Tolstoy *(1978 Soviet stamp)*

Freddie Bartholomew became a box-office sensation. He received top billing in *Little Lord Fauntleroy*, *Lloyd's of London* (above Tyrone Power), and Rudyard Kipling's *Captain's Courageous* (over Spencer Tracy and Melvyn Douglas). In the film adaptation, Freddie plays a spoiled son of a rich socialite. After he falls off an ocean liner, he's saved from drowning by a Portuguese fisherman. The child is taught the simple lessons behind hard work and fair play by his new-found crewmates. Kipling's work delivered a perfect message to Depression-era audiences. The transition of the young star's character provided ample inspiration to hard-working Americans in their resolve to bring our nation out of its collective funk.

Robert Louis Stevenson was another nineteenth-century author offering choice material for the gifted youngster. *Kidnapped*

Rudyard Kipling

featured some of the top British character actors of the day, including C. Aubrey Smith, Nigel Bruce, and Reginald Owen. Bartholomew also co-starred in the popular **Swiss Family Robinson** in 1940. The original book written in 1812 became a favorite of children all over the

Swiss Family Robinson *(illustration)*

world. Modern kids swarmed to the motion picture.

Unfortunately, Bartholomew spent much of the next decade in litigation with his real parents, who attempted to regain custody of their child. Much of his fortune made making movies was spent on confronting this challenge. A British subject, the child was unprotected by *The Coogan Act*. The whole experience soured him on Hollywood, and the public quickly forgot about the actor as he grew into his teens. He spent his adult years in advertising, and dabbled with producing the daytime soap opera **As the World Turns**. In retrospect, Dickens, Tolstoy, Kipling, Stevenson, and others would have been proud of the forceful characters developed on screen by Freddie Bartholomew.

Freddie Bartholomew/Captain's Courageous *(trailer)*

~ ~ ~

As Lillian Gish remarked to the camera at the end of **The Night of the Hunter** in 1955—*"Children are man at his strongest...They endure and abide."* The screenwriters of the thirties mainly got it right, especially when assessing the youth who grew up during the troubling Depression. Today, the popularity of young actors remains a tangible tribute to savvy performances, and the film studios dedicated to telling their story.

Lillian Gish and child actors/The Night of the Hunter *(trailer)*

CHAPTER EIGHT

FLIRTING WITH HISTORY

Charles Coburn (1877-1961)

THE PREMISE BEHIND THE FORGOTTEN HOLLYWOOD series reveals how producers during Hollywood's studio era had a deep and abiding respect for history. Scriptwriters recounted the drama of what we learned in schools and libraries. At times, the truth could be stretched with creative license, but the compelling focus on-screen was to visually tell three-dimensional narratives, sharing what we call our "collective human experience."

I personally selected actors who either had a body of work consistent with a specific historical perspective, or who actually lived through past events important enough to examine as part of our nation's cultural heritage. No actor has embodied both

Charles Coburn/*Vivacious Lady (trailer)*

measures of determination more completely than Charles Coburn. This Southern gentleman shaped modern Broadway, captured the essence of almost every genre on film, and appeared in enough biographical movies that one might suspect he really lived in each of the eras he cinematically crafted. Coburn also had great luck to appear with a number of top actors at the genesis of their iconic status.

Often confused as a British actor, Charles Coburn was in fact born in Savannah, Georgia, during the end of America's Reconstruction. He spent his youth in theater, but, his start was modest. He was content with working as an usher or doorman at local productions. Coburn became vastly knowledgeable about the inner workings of the stage, and he was promoted to manager at eighteen. He set his sights on Broadway, eventually moving there at the turn-of-the-century.

Coburn received his first New York acting role in 1901, and formed his own production company five years later. He and his wife spent the next three decades producing, directing, and starring in over twenty-five original and adapted dramas, comedies, and light musicals. In 1928, a house was officially named the Coburn Theatre in their honor. Among the actors who shared the stage with the gifted husband-and-wife team were Sydney Greenstreet, Tyrone Power Sr., and Milburn Stone (*Doc Adams* on **Gunsmoke**). When his wife died suddenly in 1937, he left Manhattan (returning only briefly in 1952).

Broadway *(circa 1920)*

He arrived at MGM just as James Stewart started jelling as a bright young star. Beginning with *Of Human Hearts*, Coburn ended up with Stewart in three films. These films convinced Frank Capra to sign the gangly actor to star in *You Can't Take It with You*, and in his signature role in *Mr. Smith Goes to Washington*. In 1939, Coburn curiously appeared in the only movie in which Clark Gable actually sang and danced, *Idiot's Delight* (the number was *Puttin' on the Ritz*); and in Ginger Rogers' first non-dancing and non-singing motion picture, *Bachelor Mother*. Charles Coburn also had the distinction of being cast in the first Bob Hope-Bing Crosby-Dorothy Lamour teaming—*Road to Singapore*. Because the film was a massive hit, Hope was invited to host the 1940 Oscar ceremony. This began the comedian's longstanding relationship with the Academy Awards.

Comedy came easy to the serious Coburn because of his vast experience on Broadway. He played it straight in the screwball gems *In Name Only* and *The Lady Eve*. He also appeared in *H. M. Pulham, Esq.*, and co-starred with Jack Benny in *George Washington Slept Here*. However, his best comedic work came while playing opposite Jean Arthur. Her early relationship with Director Capra prepared her for plum parts throughout the 1940s.

Coburn was nominated for an Academy Award in 1941 for *The Devil and Miss Jones*, and he actually won an Oscar two years later for *The More the Merrier*. Arthur also received a nomination for her screen performance; the only time despite fine roles in *Mr. Deeds Goes to Town*, *You Can't Take It with You*, *Only Angels Have Wings*, *Mr. Smith Goes to Washington*, and later in *Shane*. Coburn and Arthur's last film together was *The Impatient Years*.

Jean Arthur/Only Angels Have Wings
(trailer)

Charles Coburn (1877-1961)

Despite his success in comedy, Charles Coburn began a love affair with historical cinema in 1939. This fortuitous casting came at a time when Spencer Tracy started receiving important films after his back-to-back Oscars in **Captain's Courageous** and **Boys Town**. Tracy and Coburn appeared together first in **Stanley and Livingstone**. It's the fact-based account of the arduous 1871 journey made by reporter Henry M. Stanley in search of missionary Dr. David Livingstone, lost somewhere in Africa. Born in Wales, Stanley first made a name for himself fighting for both sides in the American Civil War. After the conflict, James Gordon Bennett of the *New York Herald* employed

Journalist Sir Henry M. Stanley

him. Stanley was sent to Asia as a correspondent. He was imprisoned by the Ottoman Empire as a spy, but luckily talked his way out

Stanley and Livingstone *(drawing)*

of jail. His most famous trip (to the Congo) lasted ten months and he eventually found his intended subject, uttering simply *"Dr. Livingstone, I presume…"* His exploits over three continents got Henry Stanley knighted, and he became internationally famous as a writer and explorer. Coburn co-stars in the film as a fictional lord in England who reminds Stanley that he may write for an American newspaper, but his travels would be done in the name of his Queen. The film erroneously suggests Stanley continued Livingstone's work in Africa after his death.

MGM paid particular homage to Thomas Alva Edison in two films. In the first, Mickey Rooney stars as the young inventor curious about the ways of science. In the second picture, Spencer Tracy assumes his adult life. Of course, Edison was the prolific inventor who created the phonograph, the motion picture camera, and the electric light bulb. Less obvious is that he pioneered the concept of mass production, teamwork, and the use of an industrial research laboratory. He also established the first movie studio in the United States. Dubbed the *Wizard of Menlo Park* (the New Jersey site where Edison labored on his inventions), he was instrumental in the creation of electric power generation and distribution to city homes and major industry. He popularly contributed to the modernization of global industry at the turn of the century.

Edison Company
(advertisement)

Upon his death, Thomas Edison held over one thousand patents in the United States, the United Kingdom, France, and Germany. Despite his absolute triumph in the field of invention, the movie paints Edison as a frequently

Thomas Alva Edison

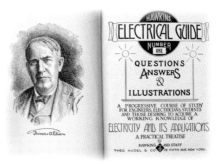

Edison pamphlet *(circa 1917)*

absent husband and a poor businessman. In reality, he sold some of his creations to fund future work, while struggling to pay his employees and his rent. One of his financial benefactors was portrayed by Charles Coburn in the picture.

A real-life issue coalesced when Coburn appeared in a pair of movies, one starring John Wayne and the other featuring Ronald Reagan. *Three Faces West* was a forgettable film with *The Duke*., *King's Row,* however, emerged as a scathing flick, making the future president a star. The original novel portrayed the subtle horrors of suburban life. The motion picture pre-dated similar works such as *Peyton Place* by fifteen years.

Coburn plays a sadistic surgeon who amputates Reagan's legs. In the film's gory climax, Reagan exclaims (as he finds out what has happened), "*Where's the rest of me*?" Only his death scene in the film biography of Knute Rockne has been revisited by more movie audiences. Away from the screen, Charles Coburn later joined Reagan and Wayne, serving as Vice President in the Motion Picture Alliance for the Preservation of American Ideals. This organization confronted Communism in the film community during the Cold War. Some of the attacked actors, writers, and directors might have felt Reagan's shock in *King's Row* after this body of supporters within cinema visited the House Un-American Activities Committee in Congress and named names!

In 1944, Darryl F. Zanuck brought the life of the twenty-eighth US president to the screen. *Wilson* was the producer's pet project, and it captured the statesman's lightning rise from his stint as president of Princeton University and Governor of New Jersey, to his two terms in the White House. It's also delicate in recounting his two marriages; how the Great War affected his administration; his uniform desire to establish the League

Producer Darryl F. Zanuck / The Grapes of Wrath *(trailer)*

President Woodrow Wilson
(official portrait)

President Woodrow and
Edith Wilson

of Nations; and his subsequent stroke. Geraldine Fitzgerald shines as his second wife, who literally presided over the nation during his illness. Coburn played one of Wilson's friends, a doctor.

Alexander Knox portrayed the great leader with understated intelligence, but the movie was a complete flop at the box office. Zanuck may have needed a physician after pouring his heart and soul into this project, which left his psyche in shambles. Consequently, all employees at 20th Century Fox were forbidden to even mention the motion picture by name, despite the fact it won five Oscars.

Famed Directors Ernst Lubitsch and Otto Preminger worked on *A Royal Scandal* in 1945. The film is an elegant look at the private life of Catherine the Great of Russia. She ruled as empress during the latter half of the eighteenth century, and is noted for overseeing her country in its Western Enlightenment period. Russia grew into a major power during her reign, and she

Catherine II of Russia *(portrait)*

modernized the government throughout her administration, dividing the country into manageable districts and provinces. Unfortunately, she never really elevated the peasantry beyond poverty, and was often sidetracked by suitors that were frankly unworthy of her attention. These common and extended noble flaws eventually sealed the fate of the Romanov dynasty in the early twentieth century. Coburn played a loyal chancellor in this grand movie.

British actors have long celebrated the idea of portraying Americans in cinema. No American actor was better at returning the favor than Charles Coburn. As noted earlier, filmgoers naturally assumed he was from England. Beginning with **Stanley and Livingstone**, Coburn also appeared in **The Green Years** (snaring another Oscar nomination), **Lured** (playing a Scotland Yard inspector), **Col. Effingham's Raid**, Alfred Hitchcock's **The Paradine Case**, and enjoyed a small role as a Victorian Hong Kong clerk in **Around the World in Eighty Days**.

In the early 1950s, Coburn co-starred with a young Marilyn Monroe in a pair of comedies that defined her on-and-off screen persona for a decade (and beyond)—**Monkey Business** and **Gentlemen Prefer Blondes**. The young actress was memorable with previously small roles in **All About Eve** and **The Asphalt Jungle**, but they lacked the devil-may-care attitude that made her a true icon. Legend also has it that James Dean starred in only three films in his

Marilyn Monroe and Charles Coburn/ Gentleman Prefer Blondes *(trailer)*

Marilyn Monroe/Gentleman Prefer Blondes *(trailer)*

brief, tragic life. Actually, he had a small role in the film **Has Anybody Seen My Gal** in 1952, a movie featuring (of course) Charles Coburn.

Coburn's final screen appearances were indeed fitting his historic pedigree. In **The Story of Mankind**, Coburn is cast as the acclaimed *Father of Medicine*... Hippocrates. This Greek physician lived before the birth of Christ, and pioneered medical practice as a clinical profession. Doctors still take the *Hippocratic Oath* as part of their solemn duty to the infirmed and injured.

Philosopher Hippocrates *(bust)*

Charles Coburn's last film tackled the story of **John Paul Jones**. In the film, Coburn was *Benjamin Franklin*. With John Adams, Franklin agreed with the officer's strategy in confronting the British in 1777. In a bit of irony, Bette Davis appeared as *Catherine the Great* in a small role. In history, Jones is regarded as the ablest of naval officers during the Revolutionary War. In truth, his real name was John Paul...adding *Jones* to hide the fact that he thought of himself as a

John Paul Jones *(portrait)*

murderous felon who was running from the law, though a court absolved him for the killing of a naval companion early in his career. While in France, Franklin and Adams assigned Jones his own vessel for the war. The commander successfully engaged the British at the Battle of Flamborough Head, off the coast of Yorkshire. His legend was enhanced when he reportedly remarked to members of his command, *"I have not yet begun to fight."* For his service in battle, both the Continental Congress and France honored his efforts. He lived his last years in Paris and was buried there. In 1905, his body was exhumed and returned to the United States aboard the *USS Brooklyn*. Three cruisers and seven battleships joined in the procession of his return to America. His remains are now buried at the US Naval Academy in Annapolis, Maryland.

Charles Coburn continued working in small roles on television until his death in 1961. This magnificent Confederate charmer was as grand as the roles in his films, but his lifelong love of theatre and cinema was simple and endearing. I also suspect he would have handed out programs and found you a comfortable seat in your own home or movie house given the chance. Our vast American history has been blessed by noble contributions of this fine actor.

Charles Coburn/The Paradine Case *(trailer)*

CHAPTER NINE

THE GOOD SOLDIER

Alan Hale Sr. (1892-1950)

THE CAREER OF ALAN HALE SR. is a scrapbook of loyalty, heroism, and good-natured fun. Appearing in period pieces, tales of the Old West, and war films, the actor spent four decades enabling stars of motion pictures. He provided on-screen acts of bravado, making him likable and bankable as the most reliable of character actors. It's almost as if the term "sidekick" was created for the burly supporting star. When he played a rare villain, audiences couldn't be at fault for even rooting for him. This is how popular he had become by the time he died in 1950.

As with most mature actors in Hollywood's Golden Age, Hale dabbled at directing silent films when he wasn't on screen. His first role was in 1911 in a Western called **The Cowboy and the Lady**. In 1922, he played *Little John* in **Robin Hood**, a favorite part he reprised a few more times throughout his lifetime. Douglas Fairbanks starred in this adventure classic with

Alan Hale Sr.

Wallace Beery, who co-starred as *Richard the Lion-Hearted*. United Artists produced this big budget picture to showcase Fairbanks. The movie studio, still in its infancy, was formed just three years prior in 1919. Joining Douglas Fairbanks in the establishment of the film company was his wife. Mary Pickford, Charlie Chaplin, and Director D.W. Griffith. United Artists creatively offered appreciative clout to some of the top performers of the day.

Douglas Fairbanks/Robin Hood *(still)*

D.W. Griffith, Mary Pickford, Charlie Chaplin *(seated)* and Douglas Fairbanks *(1919)*

United Artists stockholders *(1920 document)*

THE GOOD SOLDIER

MGM, RKO, and Columbia Studios were unsure how to cast Hale. He appeared in films such as **Susan Lenox (Her Fall and Rise)**, **The Sin of Madelon Claudet**, **Of Human Bondage**, **The Little Minister**, and the popular **It Happened One Night**. In the latter picture, he portrays a fleece artist who picks up Clark Gable and Claudette Colbert when they attempt to hitchhike on the open road. The flick started the "screwball comedy" craze, turned out to be a box-office bonanza, and swept the 1934 Academy Awards. Hale's performance, however, is really uneven.

The actor had a small role in **The Lost Patrol,** portraying a gallant but doomed soldier in a regiment held together by desperation during a fictional World War I campaign in the Mesopotamian desert. This was a superior production with a talented cast that included Boris Karloff and Victor McLaglen. This masculine film directed by John Ford suited Hale's movie persona. The opening score was written by Max Steiner, and later used in **Casablanca**. Academy voters in 1943 were acutely aware of this, and they kept the composer from earning an Oscar.

In 1935, Hale was once again linked to Richard the Lion-Hearted in **The Crusades**. His character, *Blondel,* is based in fact; a minstrel who accompanies Richard on his Third Crusade in the latter twelfth century. Blondel, also an accomplished poet, helped document the legend of the conquering king for future generations of Brits.

A jovial presence in motion pictures, Alan Hale Sr. nevertheless made relatively few comedies. He co-starred in the Laurel and Hardy film **Our Relations**, playing the foil in a part usually reserved for versatile silent comedian Edgar Kennedy. Hale adapted the popular "slow

Philip II and Richard the Lionhearted
(drawing)

burn" style of Kennedy as the duo wreaked havoc upon his character. "Slow burn" employs a building frustration at a given situation, which culminates with a sustained glance into the camera (and presumably at the audience), before blowing up in reactive anger in response to a mishap. This movie proved important to his son Alan Hale Jr., who sat on the set watching, learning, and laughing at the antics of the legendary duo. Hale's son later used the "slow burn" technique on television in his role as the *Skipper* on **Gilligan's Island**.

Laurel and Hardy
(statue silhouette)

In Samuel Goldwyn's production of **The Adventures of Marco Polo**, Alan Hale Sr. is an initial adversary to the legendary thirteenth-century Mongol leader Kublai Khan. The movie provides a tongue-in-cheek look at how the Far East was perceived historically, and by Hollywood scriptwriters. There are plenty of stereotypes to offend Chinese-Americans who today observe the film with disdain. Basil Rathbone plays a respectable villain. However, the motion picture's star, Gary Cooper, was terribly miscast. The audience could never believe his character had traveled from Venice with his Montana drawl. And, *The Goldwyn Girls* featured were pretty, but hardly ethnic-looking. Hale played a boastful rival who emerges a willing ally in an effort to retain the Khan Empire. Hale offers a glimpse of his fighting spirit and loyal nature in this piece of cinematic tripe.

Hale's villainy was well-suited as *Captain of the Guard* in the adaptation of

Marco Polo and Kublai Khan *(portrait)*

Mark Twain's **The Prince and the Pauper**. Although essentially a bad guy in the film, Warner Brothers (his new studio home) saw in Hale an amusingly stoic type they could employ when it came time to cast a project. He also developed a fortuitous relationship with Errol Flynn during the production. They made thirteen movies together, forming a friendship that lasted the remainder of their careers (until Hale's death). Their next assignment cemented this lucrative bond.

Errol Flynn

Hale was the natural pick to play *Little John* again in the 1938 version of **The Adventures of Robin Hood**. Of course, Flynn starred as the heroic "man in tights." Errol Flynn seldom lost a fight in almost any of his motion pictures. When he did lose a hand-to-hand contest, it was almost always to Alan Hale Sr., usually in a good-natured skirmish as in *Robin Hood*. In the film, *Little John* dunks the rogue bandit into a pond, which earns his entry into the band of *Merry Men*. Hale's gallantry highlights this rousing film.

Hale also defeated Flynn in an all-out battle during **The Private Lives of Elizabeth and**

Robin Hood and Little John
(drawing)

Alan Hale Sr. (1892-1950)

Essex. Hale portrays the *Earl of Tyrone*, an Irish lord who rebels against the throne. Though *Essex* agrees to a gracious defeat in battle, it's this losing confrontation that leads to his demise back home at the hands of his Queen.

Alan Hale Sr. was so popular in these Warner Brothers classics that he became the appropriate choice to play first mate to Flynn's character in **The Sea Hawk**. This film fictionalizes an English conflict with the Spanish Armada during the early reign of Queen Elizabeth I.

Footsteps in the Dark was a lighthearted mystery, pairing the duo as detective and police investigator. In Westerns, Hale could be counted on to be Errol Flynn's best friend. These films include **Dodge City**, **Virginia City**, and **Santa Fe Trail**. In the turn-of-the-twentieth-century boxing film **Gentleman Jim**, he plays Flynn's father. It seems Hale was always in Flynn's corner, no matter the genre.

Defeat of the Spanish Armada *(portrait)*

United Artists borrowed Hale in 1939 to play one of the gallant men in literary history. **The Man in the Iron Mask** is based on the final section of the Alexandre Dumas 1847 novel **The Vicomte de Bragelonne**. In many of the French author's work, he often included his cherished creations *The Three Musketeers* (and d'Artagnan). The title character of the movie was actually a legendary figure surmised by Voltaire, the philosopher and writer during the French Enlightenment of the eighteenth century. The essayist had a

Philosopher Voltaire *(drawing)*

THE GOOD SOLDIER

hunch King Louis XIV had a twin brother that he met during his own brief imprisonment in the Bastille. The jailer and his superiors candidly spoke of a regal individual kept in confinement by order of the king during his reign. Dumas later used the legend to further his dynamic stories of gallantry. Alan Hale played *Porthos*, one of the brave musketeers in the devious court of Louis XIV of France.

When working with the other 'star' of the Warner Brothers lot, Hale took on a different role. James Cagney found a dependable antagonist in war movies, since Hale had the look of a drill sergeant. Against Cagney's diminutive build, he could be comically menacing. However, he portrayed the good soldier who trains Cagney well enough to fight the true enemies of America during another international war. Alan Hale Sr.'s best performances came when the United States needed his larger-than-life temperament to boost the morale of an audience unsure about the fate of their boys going off to battle. In fact, he had a cameo role in **The Hollywood Canteen** in 1944. Other subjects in my book who appeared in this cinematic tribute were Jack Carson, S.Z. Sakall (and as I previously mentioned—Sydney Greenstreet and Peter Lorre).

Hale's "war record" on screen…
The Fighting 69th, **Destination Tokyo** (starring Cary Grant and John Garfield), **This Is the Army**, **Desperate Journey**, and **Captain of the Clouds**, a film which chronicles the participation of the Royal Canadian Air Force in our collective Allied fight. **Action in the North Atlantic** is also an excellent production about the important role of Merchant Marines during our oceanic campaign against Germany. The cast is superior, starring Humphrey Bogart and Raymond

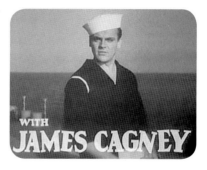

James Cagney/Here Comes the Navy *(trailer)*

The Fighting 69th *(trailer)*

US Merchant Marine Cadet
Corps *(1943 poster)*

Alan Hale Sr/God is My Co-Pilot
(trailer)

Massey as commanders of their vessels. Hale portrays an experienced Merchant Marine who serves with bravery and distinction. He would also play a priest in the wartime drama **God Is My Co-Pilot**.

After the war, Hale was featured in a couple of Warner Brothers biographies—of American novelist Mark Twain and songwriter Cole Porter. Both films were highly fictionalized accounts. The composer's fine music, including *Begin the Beguine, My Heart Belongs to Daddy*, and *Night And Day* (the title of the picture), makes the latter film worth watching

Alan Hale Sr.'s last pairing with Errol Flynn came in 1948 in **The Adventures of Don Juan**. Both looked sluggish—one because of a celebrated drinking problem, and the other because of an onset of poor health. Hale once again played *Little John* in his final picture, **Rogues of Sherwood Forest**—an appropriate conclusion to a career spanning over two hundred thirty films.

Composer Cole Porter

Alan Hale Jr.'s remarkable resemblance to his father tangentially garnered a whole new audience of television viewers who noticed when tuning in to a classic movie. On a personal note, one day while in a foursome at Roosevelt Golf Course in Los Angeles during the early 1980s, I met the younger Hale. He reminisced about his father's immense talent and the joy he derived from watching him work. I found this minute of conversation poignant, and frankly, a thrill. We can all learn about friendship and the gregarious nature of the human condition by spending treasured time with the remarkable Alan Hale, Sr. What a fitting way to remember this approachable, gentle actor.

Little John
(drawing)

Alan Hale Sr./Tugboat Annie (trailer)

S.Z.
Sakall

Sydney
Greenstreet

CHAPTER TEN

OUR NEIGHBORS TO THE SOUTH

Gilbert Roland (1905-1994)
Cesar Romero (1907-1994)

THE WAR OF 1812 CHANGED THE WAY our government permanently settled foreign encroachment upon North and South America. The British, convinced our fledgling country was destined to fail, pushed the issue over a three-year period. A trade embargo, support for Native resistance against Western expansion, and forced recruitment of our citizenry into the Royal Army, led to another confrontation. Visible carnage included the destruction of the White House, complete with President Madison and entourage narrowly escaping with their lives (and a historic portrait of George Washington).

Though outmatched, our military won decisive battles at Fort McHenry

Fort McHenry Bombardment, War of 1812
(portrait)

in Baltimore and New Orleans, providing the continuation and ultimate solvency of this nation. Francis Scott Key was motivated to write our eventual National Anthem, and General Andrew Jackson's bravado inspired a generation. His war record propelled him into the presidency. An entire age of expansion continued to the point where President James K. Polk finally spoke

Privateer Jean Lafitte, Lousiana Governor William Claiborne, Andrew Jackson *(drawing)*

for a country proudly standing *"from sea to shining sea"* by 1849.

When James Monroe succeeded Madison as president in 1817, he called upon his Secretary of State John Quincy Adams to develop a policy that could act as a proclamation protecting both hemispheres on our side of the Atlantic. The creation of the *Monroe Doctrine*

President James Monroe *(official portrait)*

in 1823 prohibited further colonization of unexplored lands on the American continents by European nations. Moreover, interference by Europe with burgeoning or existing states within our borders constituted a reason for war by our nation. This declaration spoke in response to impending British, French, Spanish and Dutch imperialist activity and the anticipated action of their protectorates on this side of the ocean. Our friends to the south, extending to the tip of Argentina, hailed

OUR NEIGHBORS TO THE SOUTH

the doctrine as a bold statement that allowed undeniable freedom and protection by a fair government. Ironically, the US Congress never ratified this widely used principle.

Jackson, Polk, and John Tyler invoked their predecessor's declaration as part of our *manifest destiny* in the expansion of our country. Abraham Lincoln, Ulysses S. Grant, Grover Cleveland, Benjamin Harrison, Theodore Roosevelt, Calvin Coolidge, and John F. Kennedy all applied the *Monroe Doctrine* to tackle such issues as increased trade among the hemispheres; the creation of the Panama Canal for use as a military and commercial passageway; a response to dictatorial edicts within a neighbor nation; and a way to keep US borders safe from nuclear threats. Modern presidents defined it to broaden our involvement by the CIA and other agencies to infiltrate threatened democratic soil. It remains the longest-running interpretive national policy.

Franklin D. Roosevelt hoped to minimize necessary and expensive US occupation in Latin America with the establishment of the *Good Neighbor Policy* as part of the *New Deal*. Peace-keeping education and military training among the civilian population became the intent of FDR, creating potential future allies as fascism started to spread throughout the world. This idea also fell in line with a growing desire for Isolationism by the United States. The added bonus: Funding for federal intervention could be used at home instead to fight the Depression.

The *Monroe Doctrine* and *Good Neighbor Policy* offered Latin American countries an initial feeling of goodwill. But as we progressed through the twentieth century, these principles gave Latins on both sides of the equator a huge inferiority complex. Motives might have been well-intentioned, but good-natured infringement started taking its toll among the countries involved. Latin Americans especially felt the brunt of the superior nature of our governmental application of the policy in all walks of life here at home. And the United States still *remembers the Alamo* and *the Maine,* which made heroes of Davy Crockett, Jim Bowie and Teddy Roosevelt, while vilifying Mexicans, Cubans, South Americans, and the Spanish.

Blacks suffered from the issues of slavery, Reconstruction, and *Jim Crow* laws. Latin Americans needed to fight a subtle stigma that kept their population psychologically inferior through all walks of life. The contiguous forty-eight states seemed to agree in the way Hispanics might prosper, much to the chagrin of the rest of our citizenry. Hollywood initially didn't help in the matter, viewing the Latin population a lot like General Pershing did when confronting Pancho Villa and his army (as Mexican bandits and peasants).

Early Hispanic actors such as Ramon Novarro, Lupe Velez, and Dolores del Rio confronted this stigma with a variety of creative solutions. Like African-Americans, these film stars battled for roles of substance, important to their respective communities. They also rejected roles due to obvious scripted stereotypes. For example, Dolores del Rio refused a part in the major MGM motion picture **Viva Villa**. Other pioneers loomed…

Charlie Chaplin had a favorite during Hollywood's fledgling studio age—Cantinflas (*Fortino Mario Alfonso Moreno Reyes*). This was high praise from the genius of the silent era. Primarily a screen star of Mexican cinema for over five decades, the actor and comedian starred in few American movies. He was also a noted bullfighter, boxer, and acrobat. A personal friend of Elizabeth Taylor and Mike Todd, Cantinflas was cast in the producer's film extravaganza **Around the World in Eighty Days**. His limited English didn't stop the funnyman from stealing the movie from David Niven and Shirley MacLaine. As *Passeportout*, he received a Golden Globe Award in 1957. In an effort to replicate his success, he was asked to carry the all-star production **Pepe** in 1960. Despite over thirty cameos including Bing Crosby, Greer Garson, Jack Lemmon, and Frank Sinatra, the movie was not well-received by critics or American audiences. He confidently returned to Mexican cinema.

Cantiflas/Around the World in Eighty Days (trailer)

Cantinflas became politically active in his own country, helping to form *Asociación Nacional de Actores* (The National Association of Actors), and the first independent film workers union. Though a social conservative in his personal life, his motion pictures were revolutionary in nature. He's credited for focusing on the down-trodden in society, using comedy to confront the status quo. Because of the subject matter in his movies, Latino historians suggest Cantinflas jump-started the American Chicano Movement of the 1960s. He created a cultural renaissance, providing a theatre environment for young Latinos wanting to explore their heritage.

Desi Arnaz (*Desiderio Alberto Arnaz y de Acha III*) was a Cuban whose family fled his native country after the overthrow of President Gerardo Machado. He began his career in Miami playing a guitar in Xavier Cugat's Orchestra. He was discovered for his matinee idol looks and signed by RKO. He appeared in **Too Many Girls,** starring his future wife, Lucille Ball. He also was cast in the wartime drama **Bataan**. During World War II, an injury after being drafted proved fortuitous in his later career. He was assigned to direct USO programs at a military hospital in the San Fernando Valley. This opportunity helped him hone his management skills.

An infamous womanizer, Arnaz seemed to constantly put his marriage in harm's way. To keep an eye on her husband, Lucy often searched for mutual acting opportunities. When asked to star in **My Favorite Husband** on radio, she insisted Desi be cast as her co-star. CBS Radio declined the demand. However, when the television network decided to adapt the program, Ball embarked on a coast-to-coast public campaign in support of Arnaz. The vaudeville-like act she created met with huge approval, and Lucy got her way.

Once **I Love Lucy** was created, the couple insisted they develop the series through their own newly formed production company—Desilu. Arnaz proved to be a visionary, making the landmark executive decision to actually shoot with film in a three-camera setup before a live audience. The high-quality result ensured the life of the situation comedy for generations to enjoy. Meanwhile, Desilu established itself as a top production company in Hollywood. **Our Miss Brooks, The Untouchables, Make Room for Daddy**, and **The**

Real McCoys were great examples of its successful television shows.

Lucy ran afoul of the government when accused of being a card-carrying member of the Communist Party. Arnaz became vocal in his fight to defend his wife. His proclamation *"the only thing red about Lucy is her hair"* was comically effective. The fan base supported Ball and *I Love Lucy* remained on the air. The power couple also made movies together, capitalizing on their popularity, including *The Long Long Trailer*, and *Forever Darling*. His womanizing and drinking eventually destroyed their marriage and his career, but Desi Arnaz should be remembered for his decisive innovations in television programming.

Desi Arnaz/Forever Darling *(trailer)*

Katy Jurado (*María Cristina Estela Marcela Jurado García*) became the first Mexican actress to earn an Oscar nomination. Her work in Latin cinema was noticed by Hollywood, and her first American role was opposite Gary Cooper in *High Noon*. Jurado was nominated for an Academy Award for her performance in *Broken Lance* in 1954. She excelled in complex Westerns, appearing with Spencer Tracy, Charlton Heston, James Coburn, and Marlon Brando. She married Ernest Borgnine in 1959, and they remained lifelong friends of Brando. She appeared in *Trapeze*, which starred Burt Lancaster and Tony Curtis, and

Spencer Tracy and Katy Jurado/Broken Lance *(trailer)*

was also part of an all-star cast in **Barabbas**, a religious epic featuring Borgnine, Anthony Quinn (as the title character), Arthur Kennedy, and Jack Palance. She made a stop on Broadway in the Tennessee Williams production of *The Red Devil Battery Sign*. The drama also showcased the immense talent of Quinn. One of her final roles was in John Huston's **Under the Volcano**.

Anthony Quinn and Marlon Brando/Viva Zapata *(trailer)*

Katy Jurado (along with Rita Hayworth) paved the way for other Hispanic actresses to garner important opportunities in Hollywood. Rita Moreno, Raquel Welch, Selma Hayek, and Penelope Cruz can look back on these noted performers with pride. In fact, Moreno and Cruz became the first Spanish-surname actresses to win Oscars—Moreno in 1961 for **West Side Story,** and Cruz in 2008 for **Vicky Cristina Barcelona**. They joined José Ferrer, Anthony Quinn, Raul Julia, Benicio del Toro, and Javier Bardem in receiving illustrious actor statuettes.

Gilbert Roland/Gambling on the High Seas *(trailer)*

The Hispanic who arguably had the longest impact during Hollywood's Golden Age is Gilbert Roland (*Luis Antonio Dámaso de Alonso*). He began his career in silent films and was hugely popular in his native Mexico, adapting superior screen productions in Spanish. He changed his name as many stars did in their day (as did Cary Grant and Judy Garland). His Americanized stage name was a combination of his favorite stars: John Gilbert and Ruth Roland. As with many male Hispanics of his generation, he played a Latin lover in his early work. He cultivated this image by having affairs with lots of his leading ladies.

Roland became one of many to co-star as *The Cisco Kid* in a few films, replacing Warner Baxter, Cesar Romero and Duncan Renaldo in six movie adaptations of the O. Henry short story. The series was popular and painted the outlaw as a *"Robin Hood of the West."* The screenplays included a few stereotypes in the way we viewed Mexican bandits. He also had a travel companion named *Pancho*. The writer created the character in 1907. Though genial by nature, the original caballero was a cruel Texas bandit and killer. The real irony is O. Henry (William Sydney Porter) never suggested he was Mexican. Incidentally, Porter adopted his pen name, O. Henry, while writing in prison.

Author O. Henry

Roland was cast in top films throughout his career. He was a noble adversary to Errol Flynn in **The Sea Hawk** in 1940. He also co-starred with James Stewart in **Malaya** and **Thunder Bay**. He had a cameo role in the Best Picture of 1956, **Around the**

Gilbert Roland/Thunder Bay *(trailer)*

OUR NEIGHBORS TO THE SOUTH

World in Eighty Days. In his brief scenes, he shares the screen with David Niven, Cesar Romero, and Cantinflas. Roland's performances in *The Bad and the Beautiful* and *Cheyenne Autumn* (with Dolores del Rio and Ricardo Montalban) earned Golden Globe nominations for Best Supporting Actor. He also wrote a poignant script (and appeared as a guest star) in 1957 for television's *Wagon Train*. Without question, Roland was a versatile actor and writer.

John Huston hired Roland for *We Were Strangers*, based on a true account of the overthrow of Cuban President Machado by Batista rebels in 1933. Although the film had Anglo stars (John Garfield and Jennifer Jones), the supporting roles were handed to Pedro Armendariz, Ramon Navarro, and Roland. The picture quickly disappeared because of its revolutionary message. It was deemed unacceptable by the Hollywood community who supported the House Un-American Activities Committee.

Cuban President Gerardo Machado

Gilbert Roland delighted in *The Miracle of Our Lady of Fatima.* The story comes from a 1917 account of three Portuguese children who witnessed an apparition of the Virgin Mary. A second sighting by villagers became a worldwide sensation. The reported miracle was deemed worthy of belief by the Papacy in Rome. This was Roland's favorite role.

Children of Fatima *(circa 1917)*

The Miracle of Fatima
(newspaper account)

Cesar Romero

The Latin performer maintaining the widest appeal for most of Hollywood's studio era undoubtedly is Cesar Romero (*Cesar Julio Romero, Jr.*). Ricardo Montalban and Fernando Lamas were popular just after Romero first appeared in motion pictures, but their careers weren't as varied. He freely shed his screen persona of the Latin lover image most of the time to create a collection of memorable roles having little to do with stereotypes. Romero was unafraid to take on difficult and eccentric parts. And he was wonderful both in comedy and drama.

Cesar Romero/Public Enemy's Wife *(trailer)*

Born in New York City to prosperous parents who lost their fortune in the Stock Market Crash of 1929, Romero happily spent the rest of his life supporting his family with his earnings made in Hollywood. Unlike most exotic actors of the day, he refused to change his name.

One of his first important roles was in *The Thin Man*, a popular 1934 film. Cast as a villainous suspect, he displays cowardice and jealousy with extreme ease. In a classic who-dun-it style, Romero is vindicated in the end. 20th Century Fox, his home studio, kept him busy in a variety of movies. He appeared in their first production **Metropolitan**, and with Shirley Temple in **Wee Willie Winkie**. He also co-starred with Eddie Cantor in **Ali Baba Goes to Town**, and in a Western about Wyatt Earp called **Frontier Marshal**. In the latter film, his character is based on the real *Doc Holliday*.

Cesar Romero first suggested *The Cisco Kid* be redone in a lighter way (while originally playing his sidekick). Originally the O. Henry short story was adapted faithfully in the 1928 production of **In Old Arizona**, earning an Oscar for Warner Baxter. Romero saw the character as a Latin counterpart to *The Lone Ranger*. His hunch paid off. He successfully parlayed his promotion to the role into a popular film series, which was later made into a weekly radio program and a TV Western in the fifties. A variety of actors inherited the part and stereotypes would re-emerge.

A successful song-and-dance man, Romero held his own with Alice Faye, Betty Grable, and Carmen Miranda in light comedies popular prior to US (and Romero's) entry into World War II. **Week-End in Havana, Romance of the Rio Grande**, and **Springtime in the Rockies** were the predictable titles of these frothy pieces of escapism. During the Pacific Campaign, he enlisted in October 1942, and saw bloody action in Tinian and Saipan aboard the Coast Guard-manned assault transport *USS Cavalier* (APA-37). He made the rank of Chief Boatswain's Mate. He continued to

Cesar Romero during WW II
(circa 1944)

appear in the movies after the war. The film titles didn't improve—**Carnival in Costa Rica** and **The Beautiful Blonde from Bashful Bend**.

The epic motion picture was put on hiatus during our concentrated war effort, but re-emerged with Darryl F. Zanuck's production of **Captain from Castile** in 1947. Cesar Romero was a great friend of the studio head, who cast him in the picture. Tyrone Power starred in the motion picture, but Romero received the finest reviews of his career play-

Cesar Romero aboard the USS Cavalier *(circa 1944)*

ing *Hernan Cortez*, the Conquistador in Spain's subjugation of the Aztecs. Taking place in 1519, the movie examines the first stages of the Spanish conquest in Mexico. The one fallacy about the movie was its use of gear by the Spaniards, such as head protection and chest plates from a later era. The film freed Romero to select screen parts over the next decade including **Vera Cruz**, **Around the World in Eighty Days**, and **The Story of Mankind**. In **Ocean's 11**, he confronts *The Rat Pack* (Frank Sinatra, Dean Martin, Sammy Davis Jr., and Peter Lawford) as a dry, comedic gangster.

Romero made a lucrative transition into television. He guest-starred in Disney's adaptation of **Zorro**. And he was terrific as the

Cesar Romero during WW II *(circa 1944)*

OUR NEIGHBORS TO THE SOUTH

head of THRUSH in *The Man from U.N.C.L.E.* He was also a love interest to Jane Wyman in numerous episodes of **Falcon Crest**. Romero is best remembered as the first actor to play unquestionably the greatest comic book villain in history, *The Joker*, on the wildly popular **Batman**. He reprised the role in a 1966 film, joining Frank Gorshin, Burgess Meredith, and Lee Meriwether as formidable opponents for *The Dynamic Duo*. His humor-laden villainy raised the bar when others later took on the part (Jack Nicholson and Heath Ledger).

Explorer Henan Cortes
(portrait)

Gilbert Roland, Cesar Romero (and others of their era) set the stage for folks like Anthony Quinn, Edward James Olmos, Raul Julia, and Alfred Molina, to accept roles having little to do with race. By doing so, Roland and Romero helped free future Hispanic actors from obvious studio shackles, and in turn, to choose stories of substance important to an entire culture.

Cesar Romero / Batman: The Movie
(set photo)

Marjorie Main

Charles Coburn

CHAPTER ELEVEN

AFFABLE FACE OF AUTHORITY

James Gleason (1882-1959)

AMERICAN AUTHORITY IN CINEMA carries the burden of responsibility in its purest form. The actor assuming this challenge must convey wisdom, discipline, a genial personality, and at times, a good sense of humor. James Gleason's characters could be gruff, bewildered, and shortsighted. Yet no actor was better suited at portraying police inspectors, fatherly figures, and blue-collar advisors of all types.

Gleason was a noted writer in early sound film, whose work won the respect of the entire motion picture community. Maybe it's because he *was* such an accomplished writer that his uniquely affable dispensation of authority as a performer is today considered by classic

James Gleason and William Powell/The Ex-Mrs. Bradford *(trailer)*

film buffs to be one of the most authentic and believable in the annals of movie-making. Whatever the reason, James Gleason is a joy to experience.

Gleason dabbled as an actor in silent films. He starred as a prize-fight manager in the 1928 production of *The Count of Ten*. This part proved to be an immensely important opportunity that paid dividends later in his career. Bald, short, and with a craggy voice, he saw his chance to remain in Hollywood by establishing himself as a writer of scripts. He's credited as the co-writer of the second picture to win an Academy Award—*The Broadway Melody*. In fact, this film was the first talkie to win an Oscar, and made Irving Thalberg the hit of Metro-Goldwyn-Mayer. Gleason continued to write screenplays and dialogue for comedies and musicals for the next decade. To keep working, he traveled to the United Kingdom to create screenplays for movie studios in England. His forays "across the pond" proved fortuitous in relation to his acting career. He was cast in small roles in many of his credited work as a writer.

Though he profited in writing light comedies, Gleason was offered the part as *Police Inspector Oscar Piper* in a series of mysteries. They featured *Hildegarde Withers*, an amateur detective who was a teacher by day. He co-starred as the inspector in six movies throughout the thirties for RKO, beginning in 1932 with the *Penguin Pool Murder*. *Hildegarde* was played by a variety of spinster-type actresses, most notably, Edna May Oliver. James Gleason honed his persona as a cynical inspector who gives his friend just enough rope to solve a particular crime. His genuine admiration for the sleuth is apparent, and it's obvious that Gleason enjoyed the role.

Essayist Stuart Palmer created the *Hildegarde Withers* series. Mainly forgotten today, Palmer became a premier screenwriter in Hollywood during its studio era. He adapted stories about famous detectives including *Bulldog Drummond*, *The Lone Wolf*, and *The Falcon*.

So good at playing law enforcement officers, Gleason appeared as a variety of police detectives in comedies, dramas and mysteries, most notably in *The Ex-Mrs. Bradford*, *Don't Turn 'Em Loose*, and as *Inspector Mike O'Hara* in a couple of *The Falcon* movies that featured the talented George Sanders. *The Falcon* was a suave private investigator, and he had an ally in the weathered Gleason character. The fictional detective also had a popular radio audience. The *Falcon* character was based on the writings of Michael Arlen, a native of Bulgaria who lived in England in the early twentieth century. Though he was Armenian, his writings had a distinct British colloquial style. These movies found international espionage a substitute for the traditional gangster film as the United States approached the war across both oceans.

Honorary Police Badge

James Gleason continued to portray law enforcement officers throughout his career. His short-tempered double take added to the amusing way he saw how folks perceive authority figures. His role as *Lt. Rooney* in **Arsenic and Old Lace** is hilarious because of his inability to contain his inept subordinates, including the befuddled Jack Carson. He reprised the same type of character in **The Well-Groomed Bride**, **Home Sweet Homicide**, and **Key to**

Author Michael Arlen (*Time Magazine cover, 1927*)

the City (starring Clark Gable, Loretta Young, and Frank Morgan). In a very rare turn, he played a streetwise mug who finds religion and charity in **The Hoodlum Saint**, sharing screen time with William Powell, Esther Williams, and Angela Lansbury. His performance was impressive despite the movie's lack of good reviews.

Gleason caught the attention of important directors, and began to appear in a string of significant films—so much in demand, that

James Gleason (1882-1959)

he eventually stopped writing movie scripts. Frank Capra saw in the actor a supreme confidante to Barbara Stanwyck in **Meet John Doe**. This was the closest James Gleason came to playing a villain. He was also Capra's choice to play *Lt. Rooney*.

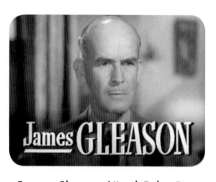

James Gleason/Meet John Doe
(trailer)

A film dabbling in varying degrees of fantasia became a great reason to hire James Gleason. His performances—a stern commanding officer in **A Guy Named Joe**; a newspaper editor in **Affectionately Yours**; a bartender in the tender **A Tree Grows in Brooklyn**; a milk cart driver in **The Clock**; and a cabbie in **The Bishop's Wife**, where he's amiable, understanding, and the knowing dispenser of advice with regards to life lessons. He was nominated for Best Supporting Actor in **Here Comes Mr. Jordan**. As *Max Corkle*, a fight manager (again), he's astutely comical in trying to understand how a deceased friend has come back to Earth. Though essentially a fantasy, Gleason is quite believable in trying to come to grips with this unfathomable situation. He really steals the film from Robert Montgomery, Claude Rains and Edward Everett Horton. Gleason is so good, he was again asked to reprise the role of the trainer in the 1947 sequel, **Down to Earth**.

The 1950s television writing community offered realism in their scripts, coinciding with the acting styles of John Garfield, Montgomery Clift, Marlon Brando, and James Dean. Due to his experience as a writer, Gleason adapted to these screenplays, both on television and in movies. He co-starred with Sterling Hayden and Frank Sinatra in **Suddenly**, which was an early cinematic look at the idea of attempting to assassinate a modern president. Sinatra later starred in the celebrated

Frank Sinatra

Secret Service and President Kennedy coffin *(November, 1963)*

The Manchurian Candidate. He would regret making these movies after John F. Kennedy was struck down in Dallas. The details and final assessment from the Warren Commission report in 1964 coincide with much of the plot from the former picture. In fact, after the events that transpired on November 22, 1963, ***Suddenly*** was taken off television programming for years at Sinatra's request. In the movie, Gleason plays *Pop Benson*, an elderly hostage who refuses to give in to this bold, reckless attempt to tear down the political fabric of our nation.

Actor-turned-director Charles Laughton created an unforgettable classic in ***The Night of the Hunter***. This movie is loaded with visually poetic metaphors, yet is the true forerunner to the modern horror film; something usually credited to Hitchcock's ***Psycho***. Part parable and part *film noir*, Laughton directed Robert Mitchum, Shelley Winters, Lillian Gish, and a talented cast of children with such adept appreciation for character; that the movie translates into a quietly gripping story. Mitchum plays a serial killer

Charles Laughton

James Gleason (1882-1959)

who masquerades as a preacher with *"love"* and *"hate"* tattooed on his knuckles. Dan Ackroyd later parodied this inscription in his portrayal of one of *The Blues Brothers* on **Saturday Night Live**, and in a couple of movies (in a fitting tribute to the character).

Robert Mitchum/The Night of the Hunter (trailer)

The motion picture also focuses on the mockery of using moral righteousness for personal gain, preceding such classics as **Elmer Gantry**, **The Music Man**, and other films of the genre. The story is stark and uncompromising despite its redemptive ending.

James Gleason appears in a small but memorable role as an uncle who finds his niece dead in a pond with her throat slit. Unable to comprehend the horror of his findings, he drinks himself into a helpless stupor. He's no match for Mitchum's character, adding to the extreme terror of the implied situation that includes an unyielding chase of the kids by the villain.

Unfortunately, the film was neither popular with critics nor audiences of the time. This led to Charles Laughton's abandoning his desire to direct in the future, and what a complete shame. Most classic film lovers now view Laughton's **The Night of the Hunter** as one of the finest initial directorial debuts in the history of

Lillian Gish (Photoplay magazine cover, 1921)

cinema. Robert Mitchum always regarded this as his finest performance, and Lillian Gish returned to movies in a worthy comeback. Gish was a noted silent screen star who occasionally appeared in movies throughout Hollywood's studio era.

Appropriately, James Gleason's final film was **The Last Hurrah**. This picture had an all-star cast, and shortly after the conclusion of production, Gleason belonged to the ages. He provided us with a variety of memorable roles in motion pictures, and later on television. Gleason's authoritative presence left an indelible mark during cinema's Golden Age.

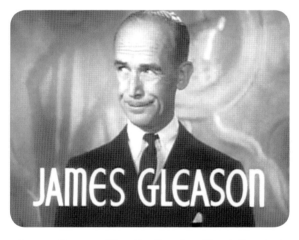

James Gleason/The Ex-Mrs. Bradford *(trailer)*

James Gleason (1882-1959)

C.
Aubrey
Smith

Frank
Morgan

CHAPTER TWELVE

MOTHERS SUPERIOR

THE TERM "MOTHER SUPERIOR" is a cockeyed oxymoron. It's used to classify a female head master in Catholicism; a nun promoted to establish order and maintain rules within the confines of a parochial school and/or church parish. The irony is she's neither married, nor a parent. But, this remains the accepted term for this maternal position, and her family includes priests, nuns (or sisters), schoolchildren, and parishioners. Her direct assignment: To take charge of a religious community of women, and her pledge of devotion is always to God.

Keep this in mind as I present three mature female

Nun in Cloister *(circa 1930)*

character actors who were "superior" in carving memorable roles during Hollywood's studio era. In some cases, these fine cinematic performers lived in households containing unrelated families. In a number of films they were childless, and many times, they played widows who survived their *golden years* with a substantial inheritance left to them by their late husband (to advance the script). When called upon, these matrons delivered as dedicated wives and mothers.

St. Therese of Lisieux *(statue)*

Margaret Dumont (1882-1965)

The Marx Brothers were comedic family royalty. They embodied a true anarchy opposing the intended direction and script, first on Broadway, and later in motion pictures. These five siblings had a hand in the combined development of audio and visual humor in film, and developed their craft while in vaudeville. They are acknowledged geniuses at embracing a storyline at a time when this style of comedy only existed without on-screen sound. Though they appeared in solo projects throughout their careers, the Marx Brothers made only sixteen films together. Early on, Milton *"Gummo"* Marx bowed out of the hysteria after being drafted to fight in The Great War. He later joined his youngest brother Herbert *"Zeppo"* in forming

Marx Family *(circa 1917)*

a theatrical agency. When Zeppo and the remaining Marx Brothers—Julius "*Groucho*", Arthur "*Harpo*," and Leonard "*Chico*"—were invited to join Paramount's family, nothing would ever be sacred again in cinema. What made their first films so frenetically funny was their lack of adherence to the screenplay, while each supporting player tried to stick to the script.

The Marx Brothers
(newspaper advertisement)

The most successful advocate of "playing it by the book" was Margaret Dumont, who appeared in seven of the Marx Brothers movies. Dumont might be considered the greatest female "straight man" in the history of Hollywood, considering what she was up against. She was always cast as a high society dowager, and her efforts at maintaining civility could be reliably destroyed by the antics of her stars, particularly Groucho. In Dumont, he found the perfect partner. His attempts to alternately woo and insult her are stuff of legend. The rich widow persona suited her characters, since she was a tall, husky, and a vocally high-pitched woman who by all accounts was the consummate professional.

The Marx Brothers *(still)*

Despite her dignity being torn to shreds by the verbal barrage of Groucho, or the physical torment of Harpo and Chico, Dumont always delivered her lines on cue. Her exasperated reactions were completely true to character. Reciting the dialogue here in print might cast the last indignity on this fine actress. One must watch their films, including **Animal Crackers**, **Duck Soup**, and **A Night at the Opera**, to fully appreciate her talent.

When MGM signed the team in 1934, Irving Thalberg insisted Margaret Dumont be hired to help bolster the script and dialogue. This move just about guaranteed the Marx Brothers success for another decade. In fact, Zeppo actually retired from acting,

Margaret Dumont / The Big Store (trailer)

secure in knowing the team had their talented co-star for subsequent films in the transition. Her peers honored her with a monthly Screen Actors Guild Award—*Best Performance by a Supporting Player*—in June 1937 for **A Day at the Races** (rare in any decade for comedic actors). Off-screen, Groucho paid her the ultimate compliment by referring to Dumont as "*practically the fifth Marx Brother.*"

Unlike the celebrated comedy team, Margaret Dumont co-starred in over fifty films in a six- decade career. She starred in the silent screen version of **A Tale of Two Cities**. Once typecast in the Marx Brother films, however, she was similarly cast as a high societal comic foil in comedies that starred W.C. Fields, Laurel and Hardy, Abbott and Costello, Jack Benny, and Danny Kaye.

What a Way to Go was Dumont's last film, and featured Shirley MacLaine, Paul Newman, Robert Mitchum, Gene Kelly, Dick Van Dyke, Dean Martin, and Robert Cummings. In the movie, she plays MacLaine's mother. How ironic that Dumont spent a career as a film widow, while MacLaine's character watches husbands die four times in one movie!

Even well into her eighties, Dumont was busy in the early 1960s. She joined Groucho in live appearances to rehash previous bits from their earlier movies. Dumont admitted in one of these reunions that the Marx Brothers were funny, but she could stay in character since this type of humor didn't make her laugh. Of course, this made Margaret Dumont an invaluable piece of the Marx Brothers puzzle. Groucho finally got her to smile and blow intended lines in a get-together on *The Hollywood Palace* in 1965, when he asked her not to step on applause from one of his delivered punch lines. He considered this a monumental achievement in his career. The television program aired after Dumont's sudden death of a heart attack, making this genial moment indeed bittersweet.

Marjorie Main (1890-1975)

In contrast to Dumont, Marjorie Main was a salt-of-the-earth type. She excelled in playing lower middle-class roles, having assumed parts reserved for Marie Dressler. By chance, it was Dressler's untimely death in 1934 that propelled Main as the heir apparent to join Wallace Beery in a variety of characters modeled after the success of the film *Min and Bill*. Dressler won an Oscar for her performance in the motion picture, and remained a big box office draw until her demise from cancer. Main shared screen time in six films with Beery over a thirteen-year period. She never attained the status of Marie Dressler, but had a steady career that began in vaudeville, and later included Broadway.

Marie Dressler

Initially cast in the same kind of parts that suited Margaret Dumont (had she appeared in more dramas), Main eventually found success offering weathered, earthy performances widely accepted by Depression-era audiences. Her big break came in the stage version of *Dead End*. She joined *The Dead End Kids* when the Sidney Kingsley theatre production was made into a film in 1937. In the story, Main co-stars as the mother of a mobster played by

Humphrey Bogart. She rejects him in a critical scene, and Bogart's character becomes despondent over the incident. He resorts to a kidnapping scheme leading to tragic consequences. The New York tenement locale appealed to moviegoers who related to the growing number of slums in cities. The motion picture also solidified the stardom of Joel McCrea, Sylvia Sidney, and Claire Trevor. Main later reunited with *The Dead End Kids* in **Angels Wash Their Faces**.

She was then cast in the critically acclaimed film adaptation of Clare Booth Luce's play **The Women**. As the operator of a dude ranch, Main befriends Norma Shearer. She helps the star out of her shell.

This is classic George Cukor-direction, and the film also stars Joan Crawford, Rosalind Russell, Paulette Goddard, and Joan Fontaine. Marjorie Main's performance stood out in this memorable cast as the tough-talking, over-the-top rancher. Again, she was the one hold-over from the original Broadway production.

Clare Booth Luce went on to have a variety of successful careers as a playwright, a journalist, an editor, Ambassador to Italy, and a US congresswoman representing the state of Connecticut (serving one

Humanitarian Clare Booth Luce

term in the mid-1940s). Additionally, Luce was a noted feminist and suffragist. In 1983, President Reagan awarded the Medal of Freedom to Luce for her decades of contributions to the United States.

Marjorie Main shared screen time with Judy Garland in a couple of musicals, playing abrasive housekeepers of varying types in **Meet Me in St. Louis** and **The Harvey Girls**. She was offered a number of landlady assignments in **Stella Dallas**, **Honky Tonk**, **Another Thin Man**, **Tennessee Johnson**, **Murder, He Says**, and a little film that

Marjorie Main/Honky tonk *(trailer)*

typecast the actress for the rest of her career. *The Wistful Widow of Wagon Gap* was primarily a vehicle for Abbott and Costello, but the studio buzz over Main's performance as a small-town mother to seven children led to a chance for her to play a character for whom she'd always be best remembered. During the making of *The Wistful Widow*, Lou Costello's father died suddenly. With a temporary halt in production, Main was cast in what was to become her signature role.

The Egg and I promoted Fred MacMurray and Claudette Colbert as a romantic screen team, but co-stars Marjorie Main and Percy Kilbride steal the movie as *Ma and Pa Kettle*. In fact, Main earned an Oscar nomination for Best Supporting Actress in 1947. She would star as *Ma Kettle* in nine more films. Kilbride joined her in seven of those pictures, retiring in 1955. They simply looked like they were born on a farm, though Main was a college-educated Hoosier.

Despite the success of the *Ma and Pa Kettle* series, Marjorie Main had increasing trouble in finding roles during the fifties due to

Percy Kilbride/George Washington Slept Here *(trailer)*

her growing reputation as a notorious germaphobe. Her increased obsession with sanitation caused trouble on sets when she was reluctant to grab certain objects, or when touched by members of the cast. Main refused to rehearse and even wore surgical gloves between film takes to avoid contact, according to witnesses from the crew. She was again a widow in the film *Friendly Persuasion*, and she made a couple of television appearances in *December Bride* and *Wagon Train*. By 1960, her compulsion to cleanliness forced her into retirement.

Television was kind as a new generation of viewers kept the *Ma and Pa Kettle* series immensely popular for decades. Moreover, the highly entertaining *Beverly Hillbillies*, *Petticoat Junction*, and

Marjorie Main / Gentle Annie *(trailer)*

Green Acres owe their success to Marjorie Main and Percy Kilbride for their comedic rural portrait of family life in the backwoods.

Jane Darwell (1879-1967)

Actresses Dumont and Main were comfortable in comedy. Jane Darwell is their dramatic counterpart. Though similar to Marjorie Main in build, Darwell mostly played soft-spoken, tough roles that addressed the Depression in the Midwest. She emerged as a natural character actress. In the end, even Walt Disney couldn't ignore her universal appeal. And right in the middle of her career, she garnered an Academy Award.

Darwell found work on stage in Chicago during the Wilson presidency. She also made a number of silent films, though she rose to acting prominence when talkies emerged. She played a widow in the 1930 production of *Tom Sawyer*. By this time, she was already over fifty years of age. 20th Century Fox offered many roles to Darwell, typecasting her during the rest of the studio era. No complaints on her part, since it put food on her family's table. Of course, she appeared in **Huckleberry Finn** in 1931. Darwell became friends with Shirley Temple, the most popular actor of the thirties. She co-starred in six pictures with the child star, usually as her grandmother, or as a housekeeper.

Jane Darwell/Captain January *(trailer)*

The banner year for Jane Darwell was 1939. Fox Studios loaned her to

Shirley Temple/Captain January *(trailer)*

David O. Selznick for an appearance in **Gone with the Wind**. She supported Tyrone Power and Henry Fonda in **Jesse James**, and developed a lucrative bond with Fonda, which paid dividends in her career over the next few years. It was Fonda who first suggested to Fox the role of *Ma Joad* be given to her in John Steinbeck's **The Grapes of Wrath**. Fonda's instincts paid off. As matriarch to the Depression-era family that migrated to California during the Oklahoma dust bowl, Darwell received the 1940 Oscar for Best Supporting Actress for her performance.

John Ford (among other directors) traveled into the Pacific Theatre during World War II to create documentaries for the government. He actually captured the Battle of Midway in 1942, emphasizing close-ups of soldier's faces to humanize their struggle. Of course, some of these men died during the fight. This had a tremendous impact on those eventually watching back home. Jane Darwell and Henry Fonda lent their voices to the production. Their homespun narration spoke to the military families, with all of the director's famed patriotic nuances. Darwell's association with the project made her the celluloid mother to our men at war.

Ensign George Gay, sole survivor of V-8 attack; Battle of Midway *(circa 1942)*

Upon watching Ford's propaganda, Franklin and Eleanor Roosevelt felt the need for a nationwide screening of his footage. They were convinced his efforts could be effective in building community morale, and raising funds through our *"war bonds"* campaign.

Darwell was less sympathetic, but equally effective, in **The Ox-Bow Incident**, a 1943 film that starred Fonda and Dana Andrews. She played the female villain in the picture who helps lead a posse toward the misguided lynching of innocent men. This picture has a powerful message, but it took years to get approval for production because of its negative storyline. Director William Wellman pushed for its development despite the hesitancy of the Fox Studios executives. Not really popular with moviegoers, the picture was nominated for an Oscar for its superior cast and story. Excellent in Westerns, Darwell again co-starred with Fonda in **My Darling**

Clementine, a semi-fictional account about the *Gunfight at the OK Corral*. She also appeared with John Wayne in **3 Godfathers**.

Darwell was Humphrey Bogart's ma in the espionage comedy **All Through the Night**, and portrayed *Tugboat Annie* in a second sequel of a popular movie made famous by Marie Dressler. Co-starring in the picture was the fabulous silent era comedian Edgar Kennedy. She also appeared in **The Devil and Daniel Webster**, **The Lemon Drop Kid**, and **The Last Hurrah**.

Jane Darwell's most unusual role was as the solitary confinement matron in the 1950 prison film **Caged**. When called upon, Darwell could be funny and gruff, as well as, tough and sadistic. Playing against type was easy for this immensely gifted actress.

Her final film role was in 1964 as the elderly bird feeder in Walt Disney's **Mary Poppins**. This tender scene allowed Julie Andrews to sing Walt Disney's favorite song from the score—*Feed the Birds*. Andrews, who was snubbed from reprising her Broadway role as *Eliza Doolittle* for the film version of **My Fair Lady**, turned to **Mary Poppins**. Audrey Hepburn played *Doolittle*. Andrews was rewarded with an Academy Award that year for playing *Poppins*.

Walt Disney

For her small cameo appearance, Darwell is fondly remembered by children to this day. What a fitting conclusion after a one hundred seventy-film career!

~ ~ ~

Because of their noted abilities, Margaret Dumont, Marjorie Main, and Jane Darwell provided sacred performances. Other actresses, including Ethel Barrymore, Dame Mae Whitty, Spring Byington, Josephine Hull, Anne Revere, and Margaret Wycherly had similarly distinguished careers on stage and screen. Getting to know these gifted cinematic *"matron saints"* might be a revelation to any lovers of movie history.

Dame May Whitty

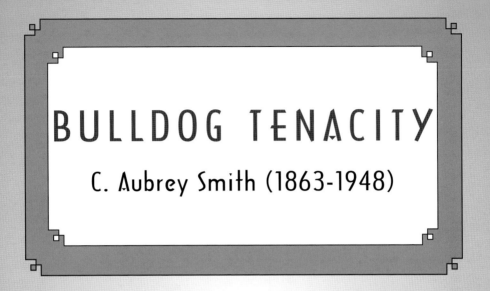

CHAPTER THIRTEEN

BULLDOG TENACITY

C. Aubrey Smith (1863-1948)

FOR OVER FIVE HUNDRED YEARS, the sun has refused to set on the British Empire. The dominion of England is far-reaching. Just study its historic expansion, global politics, and superior cultural influence for wholesale confirmation, which include language, literature, and eventual topics of cinema. One of the most obedient servants to *"The Crown"* during Hollywood's Golden Age was C. Aubrey Smith.

His roles traverse centuries of actual events, and formidable tales put on parchment. On screen, this officer and gentleman epitomized the face of the United Kingdom. In service to *"God, Queen, and Country,"* Smith was knighted for his effort.

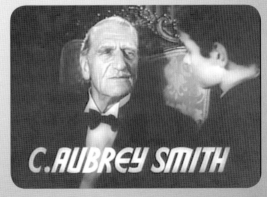

C. Aubrey Smith/Thoroughbreds Don't Cry
(trailer)

Smith began his stage career in London just before the turn of the twentieth century. He began a love affair with Anthony Hope's adventure novel **The Prisoner of Zenda**. He often returned to the adapted stage play, culminating with an appearance in the movie in 1937. In those early years, Smith was never married to just one character in the production, and played any number of parts when needed (at times both lead roles in the same evening). Hope is rarely remembered today, but was a popular knighted writer of fiction with thirty-two volumes to his credit. Robert Louis Stevenson was an admirer of his work, though *Zenda* is his best-remembered novel. During the Great War, Hope collaborated with the Ministry of Information by documenting the British war effort. The motion picture version of *Zenda* was made after his death, and starred Ronald Coleman, Douglas Fairbanks, Jr., Raymond Massey, Mary Astor, David Niven, and of course, C. Aubrey Smith.

Novelist Anthony Hope

I handed Flavia down the broad marble steps.

The Prisoner of Zenda
(illustration)

He made only a few movies during the silent era. The stereotypical British aristocrat, Smith began his film career in earnest in the thirties, even though he was almost seventy years of age. His big break came in 1932 as father to *Jane* in the wildly popular **Tarzan, the Ape Man**, starring Olympic gold medal winner Johnny Weissmuller. This was second in a long line of films based on the Edgar Rice Burroughs books. A worldwide sensation when the novel *Tarzan of the Apes* first appeared in 1912, *Tarzan* ranks with *Sherlock Holmes* and

Johnny Weissmuller

Tarzan of the Apes
(cover illustration)

Edgar Rice Burroughs letter

James Bond as one of the most successful characters in literature adapted to film. Burroughs marketed his character in every way possible, including naming the ranch he bought in the San Fernando Valley—Tarzana. Today this city is nestled between Encino and Woodland Hills in Southern California, and was so officially named in 1927 by its residents. Burroughs mirrored the life of Anthony Hope in the United States, acting as a war correspondent on Pearl Harbor, where he lived at the beginning of World War II.

C. Aubrey Smith (1863-1948)

Unlike many of his contemporaries, Smith remained a citizen of Great Britain, even while starring in American films. In fact, he was quite defiant in his love of everything Brit. He was the original *Henry Higgins* on stage in George Bernard Shaw's **Pygmalion**,

David Niven/The Charge of the Light Brigade (trailer)

his Broadway debut. In 1932, he formed the Hollywood Cricket Club, and recruited David Niven, Boris Karloff, Laurence Olivier, Ronald Colman, and Patrick Knowles (among others), to join. In fact, Smith guided Niven's early acting career. He also openly criticized British actors of enlistment age who didn't join the Allied fight at the outset of World War II.

In 1934, Smith appeared in **The House of Rothschild**, the story of a European banking family who became wealthy after funding the British effort during the Napoleonic Wars. Siding with the Duke of Wellington at the Battle of Waterloo in 1815, the Rothschild family received a handsome commission, the basis for their expansive fortune. C. Aubrey Smith portrays *Wellington* in the picture. Today, the Rothschild name is synonymous with Rockefeller, Vanderbilt, and DuPont on this side of *"the pond."* **Lloyds of London** was another motion picture made in the 1930s highlighting English resolve during its fight against Napoleon. Smith also co-starred in this film.

Clive of India was released the following year. The story chronicled the eighteenth-century rise of British supremacy in southern Asia with the formation of the East India Company. Major General Robert Clive was the soldier who accumulated the wealth from the region for the British Crown in a number of campaigns, including the Seven Years War. Ronald Colman stars as *Baron Clive*, with

Smith as a British prime minister charged with assigning to the military the task of securing portions of India and Bengal in the name of the Empire. A companion to **Clive of India** was **The Lives of a Bengal Lancer**. A fictional piece, this film offers a gallant portrait of what it was like to secure East Indian borders from native uprisings. Gary Cooper and Franchot Tone play the area lieutenants in charge of executing military strategy in the region.

British Statesmen Robert Clive *(portrait)*

C. Aubrey Smith is a major who is second-in-command in the regiment known as the *41st Bengal Lancers.*

Although a prolific Shakespearean actor on stage, Smith only appeared in one cinematic feature based on the English bard's work. **Romeo and Juliet**, produced in 1936, remains a film triumph for Leslie Howard and Norma Shearer in the title roles. Smith was cast as *Lord Capulet, Juliet's father,* who must endure the loss of his daughter to suicide. He portrays the patriarch with a hint of pathos, knowing it's his family's position that caused his offspring's demise. A real-life drama unfolded before the première

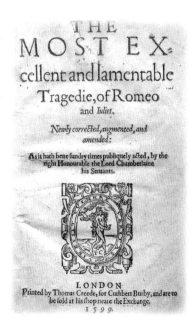

Romeo and Juliet *(title page)*

of the motion picture when Irving Thalberg (Shearer's husband) died suddenly at the age of thirty-seven. He was the anointed *wunderkind* at MGM during their initial success. Because of Thalberg's production instincts, they would become the most profitable and prestigious studio in the talkie era.

Critics regard C. Aubrey Smith's finest hour in the 1939 film **The Four Feathers**. In the movie, he's a retired general in Victorian England. He

MGM Producer Irving Thalberg and Norma Shearer

shares his account of the Battle of Balaclava, a campaign during the Crimean War against the Russians in the mid-nineteenth century. In this engagement emerged one of the most ill-fated but remembered stories—*The Charge of the Light Brigade*—which became an 1854 narrative poem by Alfred, Lord Tennyson. In 1891, Rudyard Kipling wrote a postscript, also in the form of a poem, to shame the British public into offering financial assistance to veterans of this battle suffering economic hardship in their later years.

C. Aubrey Smith was at home playing colonels in cinema. He appeared in **Wee Willie Winkie,** starring Shirley Temple; **Another Thin Man,** with William Powell and Myrna Loy; **Rebecca** (the 1940 Best Picture of the Year); **The White Cliffs of Dover**; and, of course, **The Prisoner of Zenda**. Throughout his career (and until

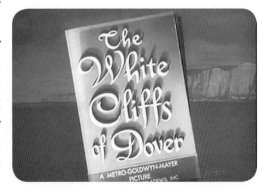

The White Cliffs of Dover *(trailer)*

his death in 1948), Smith could also be counted on to play British gentlemen in a variety of movies. *Morning Glory*, *Little Lord Fauntleroy*, *China Seas*, *The Hurricane* (as a conflicted priest), *Five Came Back*, *Waterloo Bridge* (the picture made by Vivien Leigh

C. Aubrey Smith and Elisabeth Risdon / Five Came Back *(trailer)*

after her triumph in **Gone with the Wind**), **Dr. Jekyll & Mr. Hyde**, **Madame Curie**, and **Unconquered** showcased his genteel nature.

Smith owned one more crowning acting achievement in the 1945 film based on Agatha Christie's mystery thriller *Ten Little Indians*. In **And Then There Were None**, Smith is cast as a doomed general on an undisclosed Indian island, with the story in the classic who-dun-it style that made Christie famous. This master writer of the mystery novel created the characters *Miss Jane Marple* and Belgian detective *Hercule Poirot*. Her books have been translated into fifty-six languages, and her collected sales stand at an astonishing four billion dollars worldwide. Only *The Bible* has been more successful. Agatha Christie also holds the undisputed record of the longest continuous-running stage play—*The Mousetrap*. This production debuted in London in November 1952, and is still currently running. She

Agatha Christie's The Mousetrap *(theatre sign)*

spent her entire life in her native England; the last years in Oxfordshire. Christie's name is mentioned with William Shakespeare and Arthur Conan Doyle as one of Britain's greatest authors.

Finally, Smith appeared in a remake of **Little Women** that starred Elizabeth Taylor, June Allyson, Janet Leigh, Mary Astor, and Peter Lawford. Louisa May Alcott's work was given cinematic consideration no less than nine times, with the best version undoubtedly in 1933 (starring Katharine Hepburn). Alcott wrote

Novelist Louisa May Alcott *(portrait)*

the book in two volumes over twenty months in 1868 and 1869.

C. Aubrey Smith…grand as the empire he represented. His work encompassed many visual characterizations from classic authors of the last seven centuries. Smith remains one of their best British exports in its storied history. Truth be told, he was *"jolly, jolly good!"*

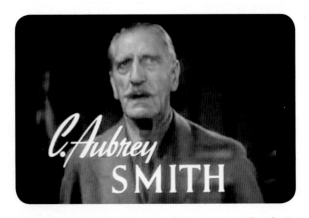

C. Aubrey Smith / Beyond Tomorrow *(trailer)*

CHAPTER FOURTEEN

A BIT O' THE BLARNEY

Frank McHugh (1898-1981)

BEFORE THE FAMOUS *RAT PACK* of the 1960s (which included Frank Sinatra, Dean Martin, Sammy Davis, Jr., Peter Lawford, and Joey Bishop), Hollywood had its *Irish Mafia*. This acting fraternity was popular for almost thirty years beginning in the thirties. Spencer Tracy and James Cagney were the hosts of these gatherings, which also included Pat O'Brien, Ralph Bellamy, Frank Morgan, James Gleason, Allen Jenkins, Bert Lahr, and a little leprechaun of a man with a huge amount of talent, Frank McHugh. At times, the legendary George M. Cohan and Will Rogers attended these social functions. Despite their dignified and comical film personas, respectively, O'Brien and McHugh were usually "the life of the party." In fact, Frank McHugh's humor served

James Cagney and Pat O'Brien/Angels with Dirty Faces *(trailer)*

him well throughout his film career. Irish eyes smiled on audiences attending his memorable movies.

Like Cohan, Frank McHugh came from a family of performers. His parents owned a theatre company, and his siblings joined Frank as part of a youthful team on stage. McHugh was

Frank McHugh/Three Men on a Horse (trailer)

the obviously talented member of the company, and he continued his success on Broadway. Folks from Warner Brothers noticed his work and signed him to a contract in 1930, as movie studios often did with other top stage actors of the day, including Spencer Tracy, Humphrey Bogart, and Bette Davis. Initially cast in a few lead parts, because of his height and comedic ability, McHugh settled into supporting roles. He worked with many of the major stars at the film studio—Cagney, Bogart, O'Brien, Errol Flynn, Edward G. Robinson, John Garfield, and William Powell (before his eventual move to MGM).

McHugh began his motion picture career in the Howard Hawks version of **The Dawn Patrol**. The director was a World War I veteran from the US Army Air Service. He assembled an impressive array of planes for use as squadrons in the flying scenes. Many of the aircraft used were originally flown during the Great War including the

Nieuport 28 C-1 Courier Aircraft

US *Standard J-1* and the French *Nieuport 28*. The aerial sequences produced particularly authentic footage for the period.

In 1931, McHugh appeared in one of the most re-produced films ever made, *The Front Page*. The movie

Footlight Parade *(trailer)*

starred Adolphe Menjou and Pat O'Brien. It was the first comedy ever nominated for a Best Picture Oscar. Studios re-made the movie several times throughout Hollywood history, beginning in 1940 and re-titled **His Girl Friday**, starring Cary Grant and Rosalind Russell. Jack Lemmon and Walter Matthau starred in a 1974 adaptation. **Switching Channels**, featuring Burt Reynolds and Kathleen Turner, was another remake based on the 1931 Lewis Milestone-directed film.

Musicals filmed at Warner Brothers were in vogue in the early thirties, with dance sequences spectacularly choreographed by Busby Berkeley. His most popular were **42nd Street**, **Gold Diggers of 1933**, and **Roman Scandals**. Frank McHugh showcased his zany style in this genre performing in **Bright Lights**, **Fashions of 1934**,

Frank McHugh/Three Men on a Horse *(trailer)*

and **Footlight Parade**, often teaming with Dick Powell and Ruby Keeler. McHugh returned to movie musicals later in his career when he appeared in **State Fair** and **There's No Business Like Show Business**. He excelled

Frank McHugh/Four Daughters (trailer)

as a comedic foil in these types of films.

After being oddly cast as a carpenter in William Shakespeare's ***A Midsummer Night's Dream*** (thanks largely to a suggestion made by Dick Powell and James Cagney), McHugh enjoyed his zenith of popularity when he starred in the 1936 cinema release of ***Three Men on a Horse***. He even played a love interest to one of ***The Four Daughters***, a film nominated for a Best Picture Oscar in 1938. McHugh established his most enduring screen character—the comical buddy—beginning with ***Bullets or Ballots*** in 1936. He would be typecast in future productions, whether the genre was a romantic comedy, crime drama, war film, or Western. These movies include ***Dodge City*** (memorable as a crusading newspaper editor), ***The Fighting 69th***, ***Virginia City***, ***All Through the Night***, ***Cardboard Lover***, ***I Love You Again***, ***The Hoodlum Saint***, and possibly McHugh's best work in ***The Roaring Twenties***. This particular role was so compelling, since he's sadly killed before the film's climax, setting up the murderous chain of events that occur as a result.

McHugh's Irish roots were on full display when he co-starred in the Best Picture of 1944, ***Going My Way***. Bing Crosby and Barry Fitzgerald joined Frank McHugh as genial priests in this

Bing Crosby and Barry Fitzgerald/Going My Way (trailer)

gentle comedy that took Hollywood by storm. It's also the only time in Oscar history one man (Mr. Fitzgerald) received a competitive nomination for two Academy Awards for the same film role. Crosby was eventually chosen as Best Actor, while Fitzgerald garnered the Supporting Actor award. The Academy Governors changed the rules in 1945 to avoid this voting gaffe in the future.

Frank McHugh played Robert Armstrong's pal and business partner in *Mighty Joe Young*. Arm-strong was the trusted acting arm of a team that pro-duced the legend-ary "ape pictures" at RKO. It included producer/director

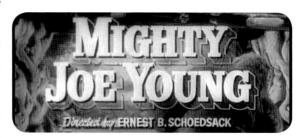

Mighty Joe Young *(trailer)*

Merian C. Cooper, director Ernest B. Shoedsack, screenwriter Ruth Rose, and animator Willis O'Brien. Their ground-breaking work began with the 1933 production of *King Kong*, and its subsequent remake *Son of Kong*.

Cooper lived life as exciting as any film he produced. He was a veteran of several US campaigns, including the Pancho Villa Expe-dition, aerial bombing missions during The Great War, and in Lt. Col. Doolittle's retaliatory 1942 raid on Japan during World War II (MGM documented this lat-ter moment in the semi-fictional film *Thirty Seconds over Tokyo,* with Spencer Tracy as *Doolittle*). Cooper's film-making experi-ence quenched his exploring spirit with trips to the Sudan and India. He and O'Brien changed

Lt. Col. James H. Doolittle

the landscape of screen entertainment with riveting special effects combined with exotic locale footage. Armstrong plays a semi-auto-biographic version of Cooper, engaging in celluloid escapades as a travel junkie and global entrepreneur.

Former Heavyweight Champion Boxer Primo Carnera made a notable cameo appearance in **Mighty Joe Young**. The movie also established the careers of actor Ben Johnson and special effects master Ray Harryhausen. It's a cinematic feel-good fantasy with the redemption of the title character through last-minute heroics when the giant gorilla saves several kids from a burning orphanage. The talented team of animators received a worthy Oscar for their special effects.

John Ford directed **The Last Hurrah** in 1958. The screenplay is from a 1956 novel by Edwin O'Connor, which was a best seller upon its release. O'Connor's books often captured the Irish-American experience, and almost always focused on politicians and priests. He received a Pulitzer Prize for fiction in 1962. The movie starred Spencer Tracy, Pat O'Brien, Basil Rathbone, Donald Crisp, John Carradine, James Gleason, and of course, Frank McHugh. Tracy's character is based on former four-time Boston Mayor James Michael Curley, who also served as the Governor of Massachusetts during the *New Deal*. In the movie, his opponent resembles John F. Kennedy. The story represents the changing fabric of New England politics of the era, and the implied emphasis on a successful personality and war record (and less on experience). In truth, Kennedy defeated Curley for Congress in 1947.

In a partial tribute to the afore-mentioned *Irish Mafia*, the actors and film crew in *Hurrah* spent many of their evenings together reminiscing about earlier days, which included a bit of Irish whiskey

Boston Mayor
James Michael Curley

A BIT O´ THE BLARNEY

to help bring their rambunctious stories to life. By all accounts, I couldn't share any of these tales, since they were laden with profanity and exaggeration. *Oh, to be a fly on that wall…!*

Incidentally, McHugh was happily married for almost forty-eight years to acclaimed film editor Dorothy Spencer. She worked on ***To Be or Not to Be***, ***Lifeboat***, ***A Tree Grows in Brooklyn***, ***The Ghost and Mrs. Muir***, and ***My Darling Clementine*** (among others). She received an Oscar nomination five times in her career for her fine editing on ***Stagecoach***, ***Heaven Can Wait***, ***Cleopatra***, and others. She collaborated with almost every major director in the industry, including John Ford, Alfred Hitchcock, Michael Curtiz, Henry Hathaway, and Joseph Mankiewicz.

This sensible actor spent his twilight years on television, most notably as a regular on ***The Bing Crosby Show***. In all, he made over one hundred fifty screen appearances, always prepared to offer his coy talent. He enjoyed a stellar career, and displayed his *"bit o'*

Frank McHugh / Heat Lightening *(trailer)*

the blarney" in many of his engaging roles. I think it's safe to say Frank McHugh found his proverbial *"pot o' gold at the end of the rainbow."* We are the lucky beneficiaries of his wonderful charm.

Pot O' Gold *(drawing)*

Frank McHugh (1898-1981)

Freddie
Bartholomew

Leo
Gorcey

CHAPTER FIFTEEN

AUTUMN LEAVES

Dean Jagger (1903-1991)

PRIOR TO THE JAPANESE ATTACK at Pearl Harbor, and most likely due to the Depression, our senior citizens were depicted in cinema as sedentary types from a slower generation. Character actors such as Henry Travers and Charley Grapewin dispensed life-lessons from rocking chairs, on their farms, or from the parlors of their homes. Sometimes they made house calls as visiting physicians in *small town USA* (carrying a familiar black bag). After the defeat of the Axis powers in 1945, folks of all ages determined that freedom included the added dividends of travel and hobby. In other words, it was time for our elders to stop resting on their collective laurels and get up and see the world.

Henry Travers and James Stewart/It's a Wonderful Life *(trailer)*

When our boys in uniform came home, the "*baby boom*" emerged. This era would continue until the Kennedy assassination in 1963. Our middle class moved out of cities en masse to find homes in outlying suburbs during the 1950s. The *Federal Aid Highway Act of 1956* was passed to develop a nationwide interstate freeway system, which

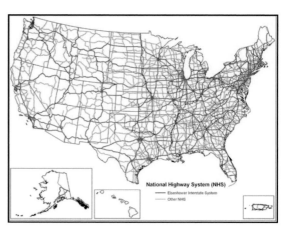

Interstate Highway System *(document)*

resulted in an increase in leisure and business travel. The growth of the RV industry allowed families to live in motor homes while on vacation. **The Long Long Trailer** was a comically cinematic look at folks in search of the good life, and starred television's favorite couple—Lucille Ball and Desi Arnaz. The long-term goal after decades of "working for the man" was a well-deserved retirement and the celebration of one's "*golden years*."

The seasonal metaphor of reaching middle age has its origin in music. "*September Song*" was a 1938 pop standard written by Kurt Weill and Maxwell Anderson. Walter Huston introduced the tune on Broadway in the musical **Knickerbocker Holiday**. When the song was used in the 1950s film **September Affair**, the recording topped the national Hit Parade. It was used as the theme for the television series **May to December**. The concept of a multi-generational romance has its origin in the lyrics of this classic.

The idea of using our four seasons to describe differing points in one's existence was definitely entrenched in a few of our pop standards throughout the latter half of the twentieth century. "*Autumn Leaves*" is another excellent example, which enjoyed equal popularity in the United States and France. Originally titled "*Les feuilles mortes*" (literally "*The Dead Leaves*"), it was later translated into English by legendary American songwriter Johnny Mercer in 1947. Jo Stafford, Edith Piaf, Serge Gainsbourg, and Nat King Cole all had hits with versions of this song. In fact, it became the title track of the Joan Crawford film with a similar theme, **Autumn Leaves,** in 1956. The definitive version, however, was recorded by pianist Roger Williams. His styling of the song captured the idea of trees

Autumn in Oakridge, Gloucestershire, UK

losing its foliage. Williams' rendition remains the only piano instrumental to reach #1 on Billboard's Top 100. Only "*Music Box Dancer,*" by Frank Mills, in 1978 sold as many records (though it failed to reach #1 on Billboard).

The actor that best came to symbolize the eventual withdrawal from the workplace to anticipate an active retirement in "*the autumn of one's life*" is Dean Jagger. Since his career includes almost one hundred motion pictures, he obviously didn't start as a favorite in grandfatherly roles. In fact, his film debut was in 1929 in **The Woman from Hell**, which starred Mary Astor. The year 1940

Mormon Brigham Young

was his Hollywood turning point when he starred in the title role of **Brigham Young**. An elderly technical consultant on the film was satisfied with Jagger's casting , because he claimed to have known *Young* and insisted that the actor actually sounded like the Utah pioneer and replicated many of his mannerisms. Jagger was rewarded with a prominent role in **Western Union** the following year. The film's screenplay, adapted from a Zane Grey novel, chronicles the creation of telegraph service throughout the Great Plains in 1861.

Grey was a popular writer of novels that depicted idealized notions of the Old West. Because of his scribbled words and subsequent movie adaptations, his total book sales currently exceed forty million. Grey would become one of the first millionaire American authors. His most famous novel was **Riders of the Purple Sage**. But, his most enduring character creations were *The Lone Ranger* and *Sgt. Preston of the Yukon*. By the time he died in 1939, he just about single-handedly assured the popularity of Westerns in cinema for years to

Author Zane Grey

come. Though his work continues to be published to this day, his harshest critics claim that Zane Grey often painted inaccurate portraits of our sagebrush history. The 1960s became the decade when Hollywood began to correct the injustices set forth during the studio era by writers, actors, producers, directors, and advisors.

Darryl F. Zanuck decided after World War II that Dean Jagger

Col. Paul Warfield Tibbets, USAF

would make a quintessential character actor, despite some success in lead roles. Zanuck's gamble paid off in 1949 when the actor won the Best Supporting Actor Oscar for his role as *Major / Lieutenant Colonel Harvey Stovall* in **Twelve O'Clock High**. This film is generally regarded as one of the most accurate postwar productions about America's early involvement in its fight against Nazi Germany. A military advisor to the film was Colonel Paul Tibbets, who was tapped to fly the *Enola Gay*, the plane that dropped the bomb on Hiroshima.

The story is told through the eyes of Jagger in a flashback to 1942 as he recalls his time in the *Eighth Bomber Command*, the company who flew strategic daylight bombing missions to occupied regions, while the British flew on similar assignments at night. *Stovall* is a fictional composite of a character that was a veteran of the Great War, but now too old to fly on current raids. His heartfelt task was to write letters to families back home about the loss of pilots when shot down by the enemy. This fabulous movie starred Gregory Peck, Hugh Marlowe, and Gary Merrill. Much of the human drama concentrated on *Stovall's* age, and his serving directly under the much younger Peck character. This hugely popular film was made into a television series, and in 1998, it was added to the US National Film Registry by the Library of Congress.

B-26 Marauder of the 322nd Bomb Group
(circa 1943)

Jagger had a small, but important role in **The Robe** in 1953. Playing a simple weaver, he foretells the important message behind the garment that is the subject of attention in the picture. Richard Burton stars as a Roman soldier who obtains a piece of clothing worn by Jesus at the time of his crucifixion. From the weaver, this soldier learns to accept the teachings of the prophet from Nazareth, and later covets *The Robe* as the symbol of a people longing to be free. Because he shows compassion over the plight of Christians, the soldier is ultimately condemned to die by tribunal, but finds solace that his accepted eternal place is secure.

Jagger started successfully retiring in films in the year 1954. It didn't hurt that he was in the top money-making film of the season—*White Christmas*. This motion picture arguably typecast him for most of his remaining career. As retired *General*

Danny Kaye, Bing Crosby, Dean Jagger/
White Christmas *(trailer)*

Waverly, who runs a Vermont inn, he longs to return to military service. Because of his advanced age, his friends at the Pentagon scoff at the notion. To make matters worse, the inn is losing his savings because of an unseasonably warm winter. Along come two members of his former regiment, played by Bing Crosby and Danny Kaye; and two female companions, played by Rosemary Clooney and Vera Ellen…and they get the idea to fill the inn with former members of the general's command. They not only succeed in helping the general briefly return to his former glory days, but a snowstorm guarantees a *White Christmas* for all involved. Irving Berlin wrote an uneven score for the picture, but this holiday cinematic confection struck a chord with movie-going audiences. Dean Jagger's grandiose confidence in playing the old soldier most likely stemmed from his previously awarded (and understated) performance in **12 O'Clock High**.

Jagger also appeared in the ensemble piece **Executive Suite** in 1954. The film starred William Holden, Fredric March, June Allyson, Barbara Stanwyck, Walter Pidgeon, Paul Douglas, and Louis Calhern. The film centers on a board of directors at a furniture manufacturing plant who must choose a new CEO, after the sudden fatal heart attack of their chairman. Jagger plays a small role as the logical heir apparent, but who is approaching retirement after years of service to his company. March steals the picture as the villain of the piece who maneuvers himself to become the next head of the plant. But, as each of the other board members fail in succession attempts, it's Holden who ultimately earns the respect of his peers and is selected as the next chairman of the board. Early in the film, Dean Jagger's character shows mild contempt for Holden's youth and temperament. Yet, it's Jagger who foresees his own future retirement as fruitful and secure, as the new CEO's vision stoically remains steadfast and true to company ideals during the film's climax. The actors shine in this well-written screenplay.

Bad Day at Black Rock is a motion picture filled with unsavory characters that Spencer Tracy must contend with: Among them, Robert Ryan, Lee Marvin, Ernest Borgnine, and Anne Francis. Though afraid and weak, Dean Jagger (as a figurehead sheriff) and Walter Brennan (as a meek doctor) prove to be appropriate allies for the one-armed stranger who has come to town to deliver a message. As usual, Tracy shines as the confronted target of wrath from the townsfolk. He uncovers a horrible secret about this community, rotten in its locale and by its moral conscience. Here is a movie that resembles **High Noon** in that each moment of the script builds appropriate suspense, which leads to a high-octane conclusion. Spencer Tracy would receive one of his many Academy Award nominations for this fine performance.

Influential *New York Times* film critic Bosley Crowther wrote in his review: *"Mr. Tracy is sturdy and laconic as a war veteran with a lame arm... Walter Brennan is cryptic and caustic as the local mortician with a streak of spunk... Dean Jagger as a rum-guzzling sheriff... Quite interesting as (a) drama... the types of masculine creatures paraded in this film..."*

President Eisenhower would sign into law the bill that created the modern highway system, and folks in Hollywood got the idea that Jagger might be a great actor to portray the current chief executive. Jagger actually resembled the former general. However, he made

President Dwight D. Eisenhower
(official portrait)

it clear he was not interested. Perhaps Dean Jagger never longed to play a president, but he spent the next few decades turning down parts that suggested a portrayal of Eisenhower. Putting his acting ability on display, he did accept the chance to portray Elvis Presley's father in **King Creole**. This was quite a departure from his other cinematic challenges.

Jagger returned to familiar ground in 1960 as an executive yearning for retirement in **Cash McCall**, starring James Garner and Natalie Wood. In the film, he sells his business only to learn he may have been swindled in the deal. Of course, his decision-making process in the negotiations is clouded by his yearning for the impending easy life that will follow. He is a man of principle, however, who eventually comes to understand this modern era of business transactions.

Cash McCall *(trailer)*

He keeps his "fingers in the pie" when offered a chance to oversee future company dealings in a part-time advisory role.

Dean Jagger really shines in **Elmer Gantry**. As the personal assistant to an evangelist played by Jean Simmons, he must act as the moral undertow in a business filled with charlatans and hucksters. This was Burt Lancaster's definitive moment as an actor, and he made the most of the title role. He won an Oscar for his performance. This movie was based on a 1927 best- selling novel written by Sinclair Lewis. Broadway turned the explosive story into a 1928 theater production. H.G. Wells was so moved by the writings of Lewis, he later wrote a widely syndicated newspaper article called *The New American People*, incorporating observations made by the noted novelist. The character *Elmer Gantry* later appeared in another lesser-known Lewis work—**Gideon Planish**.

One of Jagger's most memorable performances came on television in a rare, soft-hearted episode of **The Twilight Zone**. **Static** was written by one of the program's stalwarts: Charles Beaumont. He was known for his generally dark treatments of subject matter for the show., In this teleplay, however, Beaumont uses nostalgic elements to magically aid a retired gentleman in a boarding house. Jagger finds a 1930s-style radio in the basement, and to his surprise, it plays programs from his youth, featuring the likes of Fred Allen and Tommy Dorsey. When he asks others to listen, all they hear is *static*. Fantastically, the radio allows Jagger's character to retreat into the past to find his true love, and to re-write his life for the better. Listening to radio programs was the major source of home entertainment for families during the Great Depression, and prior to the advent of television. Beaumont observed in his 1963 published memoirs: *"Television is the substitute for what we had, and I deem it a bad one. It inspires neither loyalty, nor awe. It does not thrill, transport, terrify or enchant…"* He fondly placed these words for Jagger to recite in **Static**: *"Radio is a world that has to be believed to be seen."*

Child listening to the Radio
(circa 1936)

Along with Richard Matheson, Rod Serling depended on the work of Charles Beaumont for many episodes during the entire run of the acclaimed show. Sadly, the scribe suffered from early presenile dementia, and died at the tender age of thirty-eight in 1967. Unable to comprehend his plight, Beaumont started drinking heavily, which made matters worse. Since Alzheimer's disease was virtually misdiagnosed in the 1960s, the onset of his illness virtually tore this talented screenwriter apart mentally. Ironically, he lived the final years of his life as if he was a character in one of his ***Twilight Zone*** teleplays.

Television was good to Dean Jagger, and he earned two Emmy nominations for his role as a principal in **Mr. Novak**. The show also starred James Franciscus in the title role. Burgess Meredith replaced Jagger when he left the show. Jagger would later guest star in episodes of **Kung Fu** and **Hill Street Blues**.

Though Dean Jagger became the picture of retirement, the actor worked almost until the day he died. He had a long career and provided audiences with a glimpse at what might be possible when the "nine-to-five" lifestyle becomes a fleeting memory. The approaching *"winter of our discontent"* as presented in the writings of William Shakespeare and John Steinbeck seemed more tolerable when the idea of growing old was admirably presented by this amiable veteran actor.

Dean Jagger/X The Unknown *(trailer)*

AFTERWORD

HISTORICALLY SPEAKING, YOUNG ACTORS have always had a rough go while working in Tinsel Town. It's important to note that children appearing on early television also suffered varying degrees of problems that emerged as society evolved. Unemployment, the deterioration of the traditional family unit, drug addiction, and early death, became modern consequences of growing up in Hollywood. Furthermore, support groups didn't exist at the time to help a kid's transition into adulthood.

One former child star, Paul Peterson, from ***The Donna Reed Show***, has actively campaigned to change this sad fact. In 1990, he created **A Minor Consideration**, a child-actor alliance. Peterson has worked hard for the last two decades

Children watching Television *(drawing)*

to improve conditions for minors, and to assist in the transition between show biz employment as a youngster and achieving a normal adult life.

In July 2009, he successfully petitioned a California court to appoint a legal guardian to oversee the earnings of the widely publicized octuplets born to Nadya Suleman. Other former child actors have enthusiastically joined Paul Peterson in his ongoing quest to protect their own.

APPENDIX

DISCLAIMERS

Wikipedia & Freebase

Some text facts and photos were found on wikipedia.org .

Wikipedia content is licensed under the *GNU Free Documentation License* (GFDL), which is a copyleft license for free documentation, designed by the *Free Software Foundation* (FSF) for the *GNU* Project. It is similar to the *GNU General Public License*, giving readers the rights to copy, redistribute, and modify a work, and requires all copies and derivatives to be available under the same license. Copies may also be sold commercially, but if produced in larger quantities (greater than one hundred), the original document or source code must be made available to the work's recipient.

Freebase content is "freely licensed" under the *GFDL* or *Creative Commons Attribution* (BY), which allows one to share and remix (creative derivative works), even for commercial use, so long as attribution is given.

Photos found on the above websites were confirmed in the Public Domain (PD-US). Specific reasons can be found here in the Appendix.

Full articles on chapter subjects and themes might be found on wikipedia.org.

Oscars/Academy Awards

"Academy Awards" and "Oscar" are registered trademarks and service marks of the *Academy of Motion Picture Arts & Sciences* (A.M.P.A.S.). The copyrighted Award of Merit ("Oscar") statuette is identified as ©A.M.P.A.S. In addition, the "Oscar" statuette and depictions thereof are trade names of A.M.P.A.S.

Movie Trailers
http://www.creativeclearance.com/guidelines.html#d2:

Most trailers prior to 1976 were created as new works, which contained new material (such as "Coming soon," etc.), as well as scenes from the films they were advertising. Trailers did not contain copyright notices nor were they registered in the *Copyright Office* or the *Library of Congress*. Consequently, the new material at the very least went into the Public Domain. Many of these trailers also contained material that appeared to be from the movie, but actually were made directly for the trailer. Since it did not contain a copyright notice, these would also fall into the Public Domain

The major argument has been that the scenes from the film itself were protected by the copyright on the complete film. However, one could argue that once you cut a clip from a film, it is a separate entity, and without a complete and separate copyright and notice, it, too, becomes Public Domain by its publication. In any event, industry custom and practice have been to use trailers prior to 1972 based on the above information.

Trailers prior to 1960 offer an additional incentive since, under *SAG* rules; theatrical feature films prior to 1960 do not require residuals to be paid to actors, writers, and directors when the entire film is broadcast. Consequently, writers and directors in clips and trailers do not have to be paid, and actors do not have to be cleared or paid as long as the trailer clearly identifies the film on the screen over the clip as it is played or it is identified verbally. This information is not contained in the *SAG* Code Book, but can be obtained from a *SAG* representative via a telephone call.

National Archives and Records Administration, Library of Congress, U.S. Senate, & Presidential Libraries

Photos and pictures from *National Archives and Records Administration* were given specific permission for use in this book. Thy have been confirmed "use unrestricted."

Photographs and pictures from the *Library of Congress Prints and Photographs Division* had no known copyright restrictions on publication. In some cases, the copyright had expired or was given specific permission for use as a gift of the photographer, artist, or owner of the material. Some photos may require the condition that they not be altered or cropped.

The Presidential Libraries of Franklin D. Roosevelt, John F. Kennedy, Lyndon B. Johnson, Richard M. Nixon, Ronald Reagan, and George H.W. Bush gave specific permission for photographs and pictures obtained for use in this book.

Miscellaneous and Specific Use Conditions
(i.e., Wikipedia & Freebase images)

US government images may enter the Public Domain under the terms of Title 17, Chapter 1, Section 105 of the US Code. The photographs that fall into this category include:

Reagan/Spielberg, Robert Serber (badge), "*Fat Man*" Atomic Device, Enrico Fermi, J. Robert Oppenheimer, Bombing of Nagasaki, Enola Gay, Peter Lorre (application), Bob Hope, Doris Day, Paul Revere (illustration), Evelyn Ankers (magazine insert), S.Z. Sakall (application), Upton Sinclair, Merchant Marines (recruitment poster), Cesar Romero (various), Warren Commission (cover page), John F. Kennedy, Ensign George H. Gay, Lt. Col. James H. Doolittle, National Highway System (map), B-26 Marauder, Col. Paul W. Tibbets, Jr., The signing into law: *The American with Disabilities Act*.

Pre-1923 photographs may enter the Public Domain because of copyright expiration. The photographs that fall into this category include:

Robin Hood (Mardi Gras float), Sherlock Holmes (artwork), *Popular Science* (cover), Norman Rockwell, *The Wizard of Oz* (cover); James J. Corbett, Henry Wadsworth Longfellow, James Harmon Ward (illustration), Stephen Crane, *Red Badge of Courage* (cover), William Wellman, Lon Chaney, Bela Lugosi, Bram Stoker, Ernest Thesiger (illustration), Rudyard Kipling, Edison Company (advertisement), Hawkins Electrical Guide (title page), Alan Hale, Marx Brothers (family photo and newspaper advertisement), Anthony Hope, *Tarzan of the Apes* (cover), Robert Clive (illustration), Nieuport 28 C-1, Zane Grey, Brigham Young

Motion picture and article quotes are cited before or after each quote.

PREFACE - FOREWORD – INTRODUCTION – AFTERWORD

Hollywood Roosevelt Hotel—Gary Minnaert, photographer, February 16, 2007. I, the copyright holder of this work, hereby release it into the Public Domain. This applies worldwide. I grant anyone the right to use this work for any purpose, without any conditions, unless such conditions are required by law.

Tim Keenan—Unknown photographer. Tim is a friend of the author.

Ed Nixon and Manny Pacheco—Photograph by Laurie Pacheco, Sept. 2009. By permission of the Pacheco family for use in book.

USA Best Book Award—Official seal attributing an award-winning book by USA Book News.

Manny Pacheco—Photograph by Laurie Pacheco, June, 2010. By permission of the Pacheco family for use in book.

Robert and Richard Sherman—Photograph by Howard 352. This file has been (or is hereby) released into the Public Domain by its author. This applies worldwide.

Burma Shave—Photo by Ken Koehler. This file has been (or is hereby) released into the Public Domain by its author. This applies worldwide.

Point Dume, CA—Photograph by OMCV. This file has been (or is hereby) released into the Public Domain by its author. This applies worldwide.

Joseph McCarthy—United Press, 1954. The *Library of Congress* has not found any copyright on this image as of December 2000. This work is in the Public Domain because it was published in the US between 1923 and 1977, inclusive, without a copyright notice.

CHAPTER 1

Hollywood Canteen—Photograph from Hollywood Canteen.com

Fritz Lang—Waldemar Titzenthaler (died March 1937). Scan from book: *Enno Kaufhold, Berliner Interieurs*, Photographien von Waldemar Titzenthaler, Berlin: Nicolai, 1999, p. 9. This image is in the Public Domain because its copyright has expired.

CHAPTER 2

"We're Off to See the Wizard" Sheet Music—New York: Leo Feist, Inc., 1939. Sheet music cover. This work is in the Public Domain because it was published in the United States between 1923 and 1977, inclusive, without a copyright notice. (PD-US-NO-NOTICE).

CHAPTER 3

Warner Brothers Logo—Author unknown. This is a two-dimensional work of art, therefore in Public Domain (Pre-1923).

Ginger Rogers—*CINEGRAF* magazine, 1937. Promotional photo of Ginger Rogers for Argentinean Magazine. This image is in the Public Domain because the copyright of this photograph, registered in Argentina, has expired.

Arnold Rothstein—http://www.davidpietrusza.com/Rothstein-photos.html. No known restrictions on publication (PD). This applies to US works where the copyright has expired, often because its first publication occurred prior to January 1, 1923.

CHAPTER 4

William Boyd—Monochromes photo. I, the copyright holder of this work, hereby release it into the Public Domain. This applies worldwide.

The Saddle Tramp—Pearson Scott Foresman. This file has been (or is hereby) donated and released into the Public Domain by the author. This applies worldwide.

Texas Rangers Badge—Hartman352 photographer, October 9, 2009. I, the copyright holder of this work, hereby release it into the Public Domain. This applies worldwide.

CHAPTER 5

Lon Chaney—Unknown, 1925. This is a faithful photographic reproduction of an original two-dimensional work of art. The work of art itself is in the Public Domain. Copyright has expired

Werewolf —Lycaon. Engraving by Hendrik Goltzius (1558-1617) for Ovid's *Metamorphoses* Book I, 209 ff. This is a faithful reproduction of an original two-dimensional work of art. The work of art itself is in the Public Domain.

CHAPTER 6

Adolph Hitler and Benito Mussolini—Italian fascist propaganda news agency. If this image meets the definition of a simple photograph and was created prior to 1976, then it was out-of-copyright in Italy on the date of restoration (January 1, 1996) and is currently in the Public Domain in the United States, (17 U.S. § 104A).

Hungarian Royal Palace in Budapest —Author unknown, 1930. This media file is in the Public Domain in the United States. This applies to works where the copyright has expired.

Soviet Assault of Germany in Hungary—*The Eastern Front in Photographs,*" John Erickson. This file is a Ukrainian or Soviet work and it is presently in the Public Domain.

Soviet Raid of Hungary—Taken in Budapest by a Soviet photographer, March 1945. This file is a Ukrainian or Soviet work and it is presently in the Public Domain.

CHAPTER 7

Our Gang Follies of 1938—A 1937 *Our Gang* comedy. The film is in the Public Domain.

Dead End Kids Hollywood Walk of Fame Star—Photo taken by Donald23 in September 2005. The copyright holder, who grants any entity the right to use this work for any purpose, without any conditions, unless such conditions required by law, has released this work into the Public Domain.

Leo Tolstoy—USSR post. This work is not an object of copyright according to Part IV of Civil Code No. 230-FZ of the Russian Federation of December 18, 2006.

CHAPTER 8

Stanley and Livingstone—Contemporary illustration of the famous meeting, *The Illustrated London News*, 1872. This is a faithful photographic reproduction of an original two-dimensional work of art. The work of art itself is in the Public Domain (PD).

Henry M. Stanley—From: H.F. Helmolt (ed.): *History of the World. New York*, 1901. This image comes from the Portrait Gallery of the Perry-Castañeda Library of the Univ. of Texas at Austin. According to the collection's title page, the image is in Public Domain and no permission is needed.

Catherine The Great—Fragment of painting by F. Rokotov, 1770. This is a faithful photographic reproduction of an original two-dimensional work of art. The work of art itself is in the Public Domain (PD).

John Paul Jones —Carl Guttenberg, ca. 1779 engraver (From a drawing by C. J. Notté). This is a faithful photographic reproduction of an original two-dimensional work of art. The work of art itself is in the Public Domain (PD).

Hippocrates in-depth J.G de Lint (1867-1936), published 1925. This image (or other media file) is in the Public Domain because its copyright has expired.

CHAPTER 9

Douglas Fairbanks—United Artists. Cinematographers Arthur Edison & Charles Richardson. This image is in the Public Domain because its copyright has expired and taken prior to 1923.

Robin Hood and Little John—Louis Rhead, *"Bold Robin Hood and His Outlaw Band: Their Famous Exploits in Sherwood Forest"*. New York: Blue Ribbon Books, 1912. This is a faithful photographic reproduction of an original two-dimensional work of art. The work of art itself is in the Public Domain.

United Artists Document—Standard corporate form published prior to 1920; No copyright information, handwritten information filled in by *United Artists Corporation*. Public Domain (PD) prior to 1923.

Third Crusade—This is a faithful photographic reproduction of an original two-dimensional work of art. The work of art itself is in the Public Domain.

Laurel and Hardy—Photograph of silhouette taken in 2007 at Redcar, England by CLS14. I, the copyright holder of this work, hereby release it into the Public Domain. This applies worldwide.

Errol Flynn—Australian photographer unknown. Under Australian law, all photographs taken in Australia before 1955 are in the Public Domain. This image is (PD) under both Australian copyright law and US copyright law.

Spanish Armada—Painter Philipp Jakob Loutherbourg (1740–1812). Oil on canvas at National Maritime Museum, Greenwich Hospital Collection, London, U.K. This is a faithful photographic reproduction of an original two-dimensional work of art. The work of art is in Public Domain.

Marco Polo and Kublai Khan—Unknown Author—"*Le Livre des Merveilles*" painted in the 14th century. This is a faithful photographic reproduction of an original two-dimensional work of art. The work of art is in the Public Domain.

Voltaire—Engraving published as the frontispiece to Voltaire's *A Philosophical Dictionary.*.London: W. Dugdale (16 Holywell Street, Strand), 1843. From Biola University Library, Call No. B42 .V6 1843. This is a faithful photographic reproduction of an original two-dimensional work of art. The work of art itself is in the Public Domain because its copyright has expired.

CHAPTER 10

War of 1812—"*A View of the Bombardment*" of Fort McHenry, near Baltimore. Painted after September 13, 1814. This is a faithful photographic reproduction of an original two-dimensional work of art. The work of art is in the Public Domain (PD-Art).

Privateer Jean Lafitte, Louisiana Governor William C. C. Claiborne, and General Andrew Jackson, meeting in New Orleans to plan defense from the British invasion, late 1814—Charles Ellms, Engraving published: 1837. From the book *The Pirates Own Book—Authentic Narratives of the Most Celebrated Sea Robbers* This is a faithful photographic reproduction of an original two-dimensional work of art. The work of art itself is in the Public Domain (PD-Art).

James Monroe—Artist unknown. This is a faithful photographic reproduction of an original two-dimensional work of art. The work of art is in the Public Domain (PD-Art).

O. Henry (William Sydney Porter)—Author unknown. Newcomb, A; Blackford, K.M.H.: Analyzing Character, 1922. Earlier editions from 1916 and 1920 also exist. Published 1916 / 1922. This is a faithful photographic reproduction of an original two-dimensional work of art. The work of art is in the Public Domain.

Gerardo Marchado—Author unknown. For a work to be Public Domain in the United States, its copyright must have expired in Cuba before Cuba joined the Berne Convention on February 20, 1997. First published in Cuba without compliance with US copyright formalities, author died before 1947.

Children of Fatima—Author unknown, 1917. http://www.santuario-fatima.pt. This image (or other media file) is in the Public Domain because its copyright has expired. This applies to the

United States, Australia, the European Union and those countries with a copyright term of life of the author plus 70 years.

Our Lady of Fatima—A photostatic copy of a page from *Ilustracao Portuguesa*, October 29, 1917, shows the crowd looking at the *"miracle of the sun"* Author unknown, Sept. 1917. http://www.fatimaconference.org/sixthapparitionoctober131917.htm. This image (or other media file) is in the Public Domain because its copyright has expired. This applies to the United States, Australia, the European Union and those countries with a copyright term of life of the author plus 70 years.

Hernan Cortes—From the book *"Retratos de Españoles Ilustres,"* 1791. This is a faithful photographic reproduction of an original two-dimensional work of art. The work of art is in the Public Domain (PD-Art).

CHAPTER 11

Michael Arlen—A *Time* staff photographer, May 2, 1927. The publishers, Time Inc., started renewing the copyrights of *Time* magazine in 1964 with the July 6, 1936 issue. Most (if not all) issues that were published before July 1936 are in the Public Domain. The copyright on this magazine was not renewed and it is in the Public Domain.

Lillian Gish—Lillian Gish magazine cover of *Photoplay Magazine* from December 1921. Cover portrait was painted by Rolf Armstrong. This image is in the Public Domain in the United States. In most cases, this means that it was first published prior to January 1, 1923.

Honorary Badge, City of Long Beach—Photo by Laurie Pacheco, November 25, 2009. By permission of the Pacheco family for use in book.

CHAPTER 12

Statue of St. Therese of Lisieux—"*The Little Flower,*" with Crucifix and Rosary. Holy Hill Shrine (Carmelite), Hubertus, Wisconsin. Photograph by T. Canaan. I, the copyright holder of this work, hereby release it into the Public Domain. This applies worldwide.

Walt Disney—This image or video was catalogued by *Marshall Space Flight Center* of the United States (NASA) under Photo ID: GPN-2000-000060. This file is in the Public Domain because it was created by NASA. Copyright policy states that "NASA material is not protected unless noted."

CHAPTER 13

The Prisoner of Zenda—Frontispiece of the *Macmillan Publishers* edition by Anthony Hope. Charles Dana Gibson, 1898. This is a faithful photographic reproduction of an original two-dimensional work of art. This image (or other media file) is in the Public Domain because its copyright has expired.

Romeo and Juliet—"*Romeo and Juliet*" (Q2) Title Page, printed by Thomas Creede in 1599.This applies to US works where the copyright has expired.

Agatha Christie's "*The Mousetrap*"—The photograph by Homonihilis (in November 2006) released it in the Public Domain. This applies worldwide.

CHAPTER 14

James Michael Curley—Municipal Register by Boston (Mass.). City Clerk Dept, Boston (Mass.). City Council, Boston (Mass.). Statistics Dept. This media file is in the Public Domain in the United States. This applies to US works where the copyright has expired.

CHAPTER 15

Bosley Crowther—Bosley Crowther excerpt of a film review of *Bad Day at Black Rock*. Original full text appeared in *The New York Times*, February 2, 1955.

Autumn—Autumn in Oakridge, Gloucestershire, UK. Photograph by Jongleur100, 2008. I, the copyright holder of this work, hereby release it into the Public Domain. This applies worldwide.

Charles Beaumont - Charles Beaumont excert from his book of essays: *Remember? Remember?* (published by MacMillan, 1963)

*Peter
Lorre*

*James
Gleason*

ABOUT THE AUTHOR

AUTHOR MANNY PACHECO'S ABIDING FASCINATION with cinema's favorite character actors, has enjoyed a growing acclaim since his first award-winning book, *Forgotten Hollywood Forgotten History*—now included in the library collections of the American Film Institute, the Hollywood Heritage Museum, the Academy of Motion Picture Arts and Sciences, among others. He recently signed a theatrical deal to turn his literary work into a documentary.

A Southern California television and radio personality for over three decades, Pacheco co-hosted the Daytime Emmy-nominated *In Studio*, and currently hosts *Forgotten Hollywood*, a weekly program on *The Spa* radio network.